Embracing Parents

HOW
YOUR
CONGREGATION
CAN
STRENGTHEN
FAMILIES

Jolene and Eugene Roehlkepartain

Foreword by WILLIAM H. WILLIMON

ABINGDON PRESS / Nashville

EMBRACING PARENTS
HOW YOUR CONGREGATION CAN STRENGTHEN FAMILIES

Copyright © 2004 by Abingdon Press

This book is printed on acid-free paper.

Library of Congress Cataloging-in-Publication Data

Roehlkepartain, Jolene L.
  Embracing parents : how your congregation can strengthen families / Jolene L. and Eugene C. Roehlkepartain.
    p. cm.
  Includes bibliographical references
  ISBN 0-687-06467-8 (alk. paper)
  1. Church work with families. 2. Parenting--Religious aspects--Christianity. 3. Parent and child--Religious aspects--Christianity. I. Roehlkepartain, Eugene C. II. Title
  BV4438.R63 2004
  259'.1--dc22   2004008224

04 05 06 07 08 09 10 11 12 13—10 9 8 7 6 5 4 3 2 1
MANUFACTURED IN THE UNITED STATES OF AMERICA

To John and Lorraine DeHaes, who graciously filled us with good food, interesting conversations, and thought-provoking scripture studies for a number of years in Colorado

Acknowledgments

NUMEROUS PEOPLE have contributed to this book and the research behind it. A particular thanks to Jeff Gustafson, who interviewed a number of congregational leaders whose stories are included in these pages. We also appreciate the interest, guidance, and encouragement of our editor at Abingdon Press. It is always a pleasure to work with her.

This book would not be possible without the research conducted by Search Institute and the YMCA of the USA in 2002 titled *Building Strong Families*. Thanks, first, to our collaborators in the research study at the YMCA of the USA. Particular thanks to Daniel J. Maier, who initiated the study, and Arnold Quint Collins, who became a close colleague as we shaped the project together. Other YMCA colleagues include Carmelita Gallo and Barbara Taylor, who were instrumental in guiding the project. In addition, thanks to the Kimberly-Clark Corporation, whose generous support made the study possible.

Colleagues on the project team from Search Institute were Peter C. Scales, Ph.D. (lead research scientist), Peter L. Benson, Ph.D., Marilyn Erickson, Karolyn Josephson, Sandra Longfellow, Marc Mannes, Ph.D., and Stacey P. Rude. Finally, we thank Jason Boxt and Jefrey Pollock of Global Strategy Group of New York, which conducted the telephone poll for the study. Each of these people contributed to the rich findings and practical implications of this study.

Contents

Foreword

OF ALL THE possible Christian vocations, the most exhilarating, exasperating, demanding, and delightful is that of parent.

Not long ago someone emerged from my Sunday service saying, "Why must we begin every service with a Prayer of Confession? Those are not my sins. A prayer of confession of sin every Sunday seems excessive." As her pastor, I replied, "Maybe you don't have to confess sins regularly. However, many of us are parents, and we really, really need a confession of sin anytime we can get it."

And I meant it. As a parent, despite our well-intentioned efforts, there is always much sin to confess, the sins done and left undone, the good that we would do for our children that we do not do, and all the rest. Thus, being a parent, or a child, might be seen as the Christian vocation that specializes in forgiving others and receiving forgiveness from others. Most of the really interesting damage that is done to us in life, and nearly all of the good, comes to us through our parents. And most of my really serious mistakes and certainly any good that I will have done in this life, are due to my being called to be a parent.

Therefore, *we need help!* Intellectual, emotional, and spiritual demands of parenting are huge. Those demands are intimidating for any parent, but particularly for any parent who would be Christian. For those of us who are Christian, we feel that we are parents not only because God gave us children but also because God gave us the vocation to care for, nurture, guide, sustain, protect, and endure children. We believe that we are doing this parenting not only for the sake of our children but also for the glory of God. Thus we need resources larger than our own. We need skills. We need a vision that our efforts to be a good parent are part of God's larger work in the world.

At last, here is informed, wise, and practical guidance for parents who would be Christians and Christians who would be parents. Building upon the guidance received through Search Institute's research in congregations and with parents, Jolene and Eugene Roehlkepartain have produced a wonderfully useful and encouraging book. *Embracing Parents* is just what we churches need to help our parents fulfill our vocation. The insights contained herein, are for churches who take seriously their responsibility to "equip the saints" (Ephesians 4:12). For all parents who would be saints, this book contains some wonderfully comforting messages: *You are not alone. Your struggles are not peculiar to your family. Your church is a marvelous resource for your vocation as a parent. Already, within your congregation, are the resources you need to succeed at this vocation. Here is a vocation that is worth doing, and with God's help can be done well.*

The Puritans loved to refer to the family as "a little church within the church." The family, in its daily interactions, becomes a wonderful rationale for the essential need of the church. The vision, forgiveness, support, wisdom, and love that the congregation offers families are just the gifts that families need in order to succeed. The Roehlkepartains have moved from an assessment of our needs as parents to quite specific ways that churches can help. They also give many encouraging examples of congregations who have taken their role as supporters of parents quite seriously. Through this book not only will parents be renewed in their vocation but all the rest of us in the church will receive authorization and validation of our ministry of encouragement of parents. Right at the beginning, the Roehlkepartains show us that "most parents are going it alone." That is a devastating insight. The work of a parent is simply too demanding to "go it alone." And yet it is also a word of encouragement to the church. Most of our congregations already have all that we need in order to be helpful to parents. What is lacking is a solid base of information about what is needed by parents and specific insights about how we can help. And this book does just that.

Last Sunday I did something that is typical within our congregation. I baptized a baby, the daughter of two young parents. The parents arose within the service and quite nervously came forward, standing at the baptismal font with their baby, ready to make the promises of baptism. If I am not mistaken, they had a look of suppressed terror on their faces. I took this as a sign of their intelligence.

At the beginning of the ritual I said to them and to the congregation, "John and Mary are wonderful people. Now they have a wonderful baby. John and Mary have many great gifts, but they do not have all the gifts they need to be parents of a Christian."

I continued, "The church does not believe in single-parent families. The church just doesn't think that one person, standing alone, has all that he or she needs to be a Christian parent. Fortunately, the church also disbelieves the efficacy of two-parent families. John and Mary are great people, but they are not good enough to raise a Christian by themselves. Therefore we have this ritual called baptism. In this rite, the church says to you, 'You don't have to do this by yourselves. God has sent us to help you raise this child in the faith.' In this rite, we adopt your child, we hear with great joy God say to us that this child is our responsibility. We will stand with you, sometimes stand in for you, and give you what you need to fulfill this vocation to which God has called you."

After the service, someone said to me, "I was deeply moved by your remarks just before the baptism. Thanks for reminding us of the promises we make at baptism."

I didn't have time to say to this person standing there in the church door, but it ought to be said: *Thanks to my reading of* Embracing Parents.

William H. Willimon
Dean of the Chapel and Professor of Christian Ministry
Duke University
Durham, North Carolina
Week after Easter, 2003

Introduction

Making Families a Priority

*H*OW BROAD IS your family ministry? In many congregations, family ministry is more about children than it is about families. Congregations typically tout a nursery, religious education for children, youth activities, and an occasional family activity as its family ministry. These are all essential, but many family ministries overlook important members of the family: the parents.

How can your congregation help parents? The way you answer that question determines not only how children can grow up well but also how parents can develop as individuals. Too many parents are merely surviving. Your congregation can help them thrive—not only as parents but also as individual Christians and partners in ministry.

When Maurice Graham was associate pastor of Bon Air Baptist Church in Richmond, Virginia, he said, "Churches are already doing a lot to help families, but we've got to do more." He contends that congregations must offer more training in parenting skills, coordinate more parent support groups, and encourage parents to be open about their true feelings about parenting.[1]

The Pulse of Parents Today

You can't minister to parents effectively, however, if you don't know what they're thinking, experiencing, and trying to change. To understand parents more fully, researchers[2] at

Search Institute and YMCA of the USA conducted a poll of 1,005 parents in the United States.[3] As part of the research team for that study, we also interviewed parents and talked with congregational and community leaders to find out how they're effectively helping parents. Through the poll, we discovered five key findings:

> Finding 1: Most parents are going it alone.
> Finding 2: Many parents lack a strong relationship with a spouse or partner.
> Finding 3: Many parents feel successful as parents most of the time.
> Finding 4: Most parents face ongoing challenges.
> Finding 5: Many things that would help parents are easy things others can do.

This study found that most of the parents surveyed are working hard as parents, despite little support from family, friends, and their community. Rather than focusing on what parents do wrong (which is the norm in current research), we asked parents about their own sense of success and what they need to be effective parents.

The Role of Your Congregation

This study invites your congregation to rethink how you engage parents by focusing on building the kinds of relationships, opportunities, and environments where parents feel surrounded with allies and partners in raising children and adolescents. Many congregations are doing many things right, but this study suggests ways for congregations to be even more effective.

Your congregation can provide:

• *A safe haven for parents*—Because many parents are going it alone and feel overwhelmed, your congregation can become a place of safety and refuge for parents. Your congregation can affirm parents in what they're already doing right and recharge their batteries so they can fulfill their important role. Parents find safety when a congregation accepts their current situation and helps them to make the most of that situation.

One woman, a grandmother, said she would hesitate to tell people in some congregations about her son divorcing her daughter-in-law because of the risk of being judged. She says it's hard to put yourself on the line as a parent and as a member of a congregation. "You risk being judged twice," she says. Yet she has gained clarity about the situation for herself, even though it may be controversial to others. "My daughter-in-law is a single parent. My son divorced her; I didn't divorce her."

Many congregations today talk about creating a safe, physical environment for parents, children, and youth. It's time to begin talking about how to develop a safe emotional environment for individuals, too. No one wants to come to a congregation to be judged. Part of the reason parents come to a congregation is to help them grow in faith and to be with

A CONGREGATION SUCCESS STORY

Ministering to Parents, Kids, and Families

In Lawrence, Massachusetts, the Spanish Evangelical Church offers family nights every Friday night. Families eat together and have a 30-minute family time before separating for 90 minutes for enrichment activities. Parents can choose from a number of workshops, such as "Dare to Be a Parent," "Help, I Need a Ref," "It Is We, But Really, It's Only Me," and "Did You Say Sex?"

On the last weekend of the month, the congregation offers either a family service project or a family outing. These opportunities, led by a husband-and-wife ministry team, also encourage parents to follow the "1, 1, 2, & 2" principle: one marriage retreat a year, one couple check-up day a year, two family service projects a year, and two family outings per year.

7

RESEARCH INSIGHTS

How Parents Handle the Daily Challenges of Parenting

When we asked 1,005 parents how well they deal with the daily issues and challenges that come with being a parent, here is what parents said:

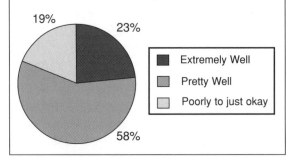

- 19%
- 23%
- 58%

- Extremely Well
- Pretty Well
- Poorly to just okay

people who believe in them.

- *A caring community for parents*—This study clearly shows that parents want to connect with others in meaningful ways but that they have few opportunities to do so. Your congregation is an intergenerational community that has much to offer parents. By encouraging members and congregational leaders to get to know parents, these relationships will help parents feel more supported and nurtured. When parents are part of a caring community, they also will know to whom to turn when parenting becomes difficult.

"The role of the church is to be sure that everyone has someone to call when they need to," says Diana Garland, editor of *Family Ministry*. " 'God sets the lonely in families,' says Psalm 68, and we are about God's work in this lonely world. Perhaps this is one of the most significant challenges of family ministry."[4]

- *Positive activities that engage and challenge parents*—This study shows that parents generally value informal, personal forms of support more than programmatic supports. This doesn't mean you should stop providing programs for parents, but the study does suggest that it may be helpful to rethink these programs so that they help parents connect with each other and with other people in your congregation.

"Congregations have to move beyond offering programmatic innovations if they want to sustain themselves as vital faith communities," says Penny Edgell Becker of Cornell University. "What church members find most compelling, what causes them to make the time for church in the context of a busy life, is the sense that they get something there that they get nowhere else, something worth making a commitment to."[5]

• *Clear values, beliefs, and commitments that guide parents*—Congregations are one of the few places in our society that articulate and teach positive values, beliefs, and meaningful commitments. These values, beliefs, and commitments help parents teach their children and teenagers to make wise and healthy choices. When congregations partner with parents, they can help parents and their children find purpose and

A CONGREGATION SUCCESS STORY

Providing Many Opportunities for Parents to Grow

Parents and families are nurtured in many ways by University United Methodist Church in Chapel Hill, North Carolina. The congregation offers parent enrichment seminars to help parents learn and develop even more effective parenting skills. In addition, the congregation also provides:

• a morning fellowship for mothers with toddlers and infants to come together, talk, and have devotions together. Blankets are spread on the floor, welcoming the young children as well;

• a 12-hour workshop for engaged couples so they can communicate better, understand their relationship more fully, and address problems more effectively;

• a parent-involved preschool program that meets two or three mornings a week;

• a cradle cross and a rose placed on the altar during worship services following the birth of a child;

• a nurturing program for families with babies to help them adjust as a new family.

9

RESEARCH INSIGHTS

Parents' Openness to Learning

When we asked 1,005 parents how true is: "There is always more for me to learn about being a good parent," here is what they said:

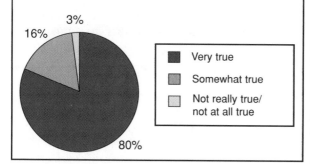

3%
16%

Very true
Somewhat true
Not really true/
not at all true

80%

meaning in life based on moral and ethical principles. With the complexity of life today, a congregation can be a prophetic voice in teaching the difference between right and wrong while also helping individuals to respond with integrity to the many shades of gray.

• *An invitation to ministry*—Parents are not primarily objects of a congregation's ministry. They are subjects—contributors to the mission of the church, not only through their involvement in congregational life but also as they nurture their children. By emphasizing and unleashing the strengths of parents, congregations not only help parents be better parents but also equip parents to live out their calling to help their children grow in body, mind, and spirit.

A Framework to Guide Parents

This study of 1,005 parents across the United States not only provides information about the state of parents today but also ties into a research framework that reveals how parents can best help their children grow up well. The developmental asset framework, which Search Institute developed in 1989, identifies the key building blocks that children and teenagers need to grow up to be competent, caring individuals. Surveys of almost 2 million young people in the United States and Canada show that the more developmental assets young people have:

• *the less likely they will try dangerous things*—Young people who have more developmental assets are less likely to drink alcohol, use drugs, have sexual intercourse as teenagers, skip school, and do 20 other risky behaviors. Parents often worry about keeping their children from doing dangerous things, and the developmental asset framework shows them how.

• *the more likely they will act in positive ways*—Young people who have more developmental assets are more likely to succeed in school, help others, and value diversity. Search Institute researchers have measured eight specific behaviors, which they call thriving indicators, that increase as the number of developmental assets goes up. Young people with more developmental assets are also more likely to make religion and spirituality a priority in their lives.

> ## A CONGREGATION SUCCESS STORY
>
> ### *Support Groups for All Kinds of Parents*
>
> Mariners Church in Irvine, California, works to connect parents with one another through many different support groups. The congregation creates small groups for teenagers and then links the parents of those teenagers together. Parents of college-age students get together for Bible study and support. Parents wanting to find parents who live near them can join a Bible study home group with parents in their neighborhood.

• *the more likely they will bounce back from difficulties*—Sometimes bad things happen to young people. What helps young people rebound after a traumatic event or a difficult situation? Developmental assets. The more developmental assets that young people have, the more likely they will get up from being knocked down and try again. Researchers call this ability *resiliency.*

Chapter 6 examines the developmental asset framework in depth and shows specific ways your congregation can teach these developmental assets to parents while also building them in the children and teenagers of your congregation.

A Practical Guide for Helping Parents

Embracing Parents is a practical tool to help your congregation recognize and unleash your capacity to provide what parents need to succeed. In addition to reporting the results of this study of 1,005 parents across the United States, this book suggests specific strategies and ideas for how to support, encourage, challenge, and teach parents so they raise responsible, caring children and teenagers.

Chapters 1 through 5 examine each of the five findings of this national study, giving in-depth results of the findings and providing creative ways that congregations can address each one. We have developed charts and graphs to illustrate some of the findings, which you will find in boxes throughout the book titled "Research Insights." We also have highlighted a number of congregations who are successfully ministering to parents and their families. These can be found in boxes titled "A Congregation Success Story."

Chapter 6 highlights a new congregational survey that your members can take to identify their priorities and your congregation's strengths for nurturing parents, children, youth, and families. This chapter also includes survey results from congregations that piloted the survey.

In chapter 7 you can see how congregations are transforming themselves to be caring communities for parents, children, and youth. By using the developmental asset framework developed by Search Institute, many congregations have created innovative ways that have attracted and retained families.

In addition to solid information, this book also has an appendix and a list of helpful resources. The appendix includes the lists of developmental assets for five different age groups: infants, toddlers, preschoolers, elementary-age children, and middle and high school young people. Congregational leaders, nursery workers, Christian education leaders, committee chairs, youth workers, and family ministers all have found these lists to be invaluable for their critical work with parents, children, and youth.

The Difference Your Congregation Can Make

Your congregation has the power to influence parents and their children in positive ways. When congregational leaders and members help parents, parents can more easily raise their children and teenagers well.

Your congregation also has the power to create a strong web of support for parents and their children. Some individuals will make your congregation a welcoming place by going out of their way to greet parents. Others will get to know parents and become their key allies. A few will connect parents with helpful individuals and organizations. All of these important gestures make a difference for parents.

Your congregation can do more than you think in helping parents. All it takes is some creative thinking in response to this study of 1,005 parents. All it requires is the faith that what you do for parents really does matter.

Chapter 1

Finding #1: Most Parents Are Going It Alone

MANY PARENTS ARE raising their children all by themselves. The U.S. Census reports that one of three families is headed by one parent, instead of two.[1] When Search Institute interviewed parents across the United States, researchers learned that not only are single parents going it alone but so are many married parents. A number of married parents are not getting adequate help from their spouse, much less from others in their families and communities.

Research shows that parents are more effective when they have the support and encouragement of those around them.[2] Whether the support comes from a spouse; another adult family member; extended family, friends, or people within the community—or best of all, all of these places—that support makes a big difference.

Why Parents Shouldn't Do It All Alone

Despite public perception that parents should be solely responsible for raising kids and are doing a poor job of parenting,[3] research clearly shows that those who have strong, supportive connections are more likely to parent better and have better relationships with their children. In addition, when parents are isolated, they are more likely to neglect their kids or abuse them.[4]

Through its research and public leadership, Search Institute has been advocating that people begin to see all kids as their kids, and avoid the my-kids-versus-your-kids mentality. Individuals throughout our society should take a role in raising children and giving parents the support they need. Congregations have an important role to play, as do congregational leaders and members.

Adding this role to the many that your congregation, leaders, and members already have may seem daunting, but this role doesn't need to be overwhelming or exhausting. Congregations that have taken on this new role have found that not only do young people and parents benefit but so does the congregation and those in it.

"This is what the church is about," says Mark McCormick, a Roman Catholic priest in Hot Springs, South Dakota. He contends that any role the congregation can play in galvanizing the community for caring for parents and their kids "is why we are here."[5]

Parents Turn to Family for Support

In polling 1,005 parents across the United States, we asked parents whether they had access to three potential sources of parenting help, support, or advice. We inquired about immediate or extended family, friends, and community resources. What we discovered is that most parents surveyed rarely seek support about parenting from any of these three sources of support.

When parents do turn to others for support, they're most likely to turn to immediate or extended family. More than one third of the parents interviewed said that it was "very true" that they turned to family members, making the family the most common source of support. Only 25 percent said that it was "not true" that they turned to immediate or extended family.

We found differences between fathers and mothers and also between African American parents and white parents.

Mothers (40%) are more likely to seek out the support of immediate or extended family than fathers (32%). African American parents (48%) also are more apt to turn to family members for support than white parents (35%).

Parents Seek Support from Their Friends

Parents who were surveyed said that friends were the second most common source of support. Twenty percent of parents interviewed said it was "very true" that they turned to their friends for parenting support. Thirty-four percent revealed that they never sought out their friends for support for this aspect of their lives.

Mothers are much more likely to talk to their friends and get their support for parenting than fathers are. Twenty-six percent of mothers surveyed say they do this, compared to only 11 percent of fathers. African American parents also are more apt to talk to friends for parenting support than white parents. While 25 percent of African American parents seek out the support of their friends, only 19 percent of white parents do.

Parents who attend a congregation on a regular basis (at least monthly) are much more apt to turn to friends for parenting support than parents who never go to church. The difference between parents who attend a congregation regularly and those who don't go at all is even wider when you look at those who say it is "not true" that they turn to friends for support. Thirty-one percent of parents who attend a congregation on a regular basis say it is "not true" that they seek out a friend for parenting support compared to 44 percent of parents who never attend.

Parents Find Support Through
Community Resources

The type of support that parents are least likely to turn to for help and advice is a community resource. Only 11 percent

A CONGREGATION SUCCESS STORY

A Night Out for Parents

Once a month, parents at Clarendon United Methodist Church in Arlington, Virginia, can go out for dinner, catch a movie, or just simply relax. The congregation offers child care from 4:00 P.M. to 8:00 P.M. on a Saturday. Parents pack a bag dinner for their children, and the congregation charges $10 per child up to $30 for a family with three or more children. For parents who often feel that they're going it alone and never have time to themselves, this congregation offers a critical ministry in giving parents a few hours off.

For stay-at-home parents, Hillside Christian Church in Wichita, Kansas, offers a weekly time every Friday during the school year. Between 9:30 A.M. and 1:30 P.M., parents who have preregistered their children can take time to catch up on things they need to do while the congregation provides a positive learning experience for young children.

of parents surveyed say it is "very true" that they seek parenting support from community resources. Sixty-three percent said it was "not true" that they tap into this form of support.

African American parents are much more likely than white parents to use community resources for parenting support. We found that 19 percent of African American parents say that it is "very true" that they seek community resource support for their parenting compared to only 10 percent of white parents.

Differences also exist between mothers and fathers, although these differences are not as great as other sources of support. Twelve percent of mothers say it is "very true" that they turn to community resources for support whereas only 8 percent of fathers do.

When you look at highly religious parents (those who attend a congregation at least weekly), 58 percent say they do not turn to community resources for parenting support. In contrast, 74 percent of unchurched parents surveyed say they do not seek support from community resources. Although highly religious parents are more open to receiving support from community resources (which include congregations), many still are not getting the support they need. Only 13 percent say it is "very true" that they turn to community resources for parenting support.

Few Parents Use Multiple Sources of Support

Since we asked parents about three major sources of parenting support (immediate or extended family, friends, and community resources), we then calculated the proportion of parents who regularly sought support from one, two, or three of these potential parenting resources. We found that 53 percent of parents surveyed didn't turn to any of the three sources of support and only 4 percent seek out all three.

About one of the three parents surveyed (31%) turn to one of three sources of support. Only 11 percent turn to two of the three supports.

Additional analysis reveals that the number of sources of support that parents have affects how well they parent. Of parents who turned to two or three of the three sources of support, 55 percent said they parented in ways that were beneficial to their children. This compares to only 35 percent of those who don't receive any support and 37 percent who turn to only one source of support.

Parents Want to Grow and Learn

Most parents are open to learning more about parenting. Of those polled, 80 percent said there is always something more they can learn about being a good parent.

We discovered that all groups of parents are open to learning more. African American parents, white parents, and parents of all socioeconomic groups said there is always more to learn. Eighty-four percent of mothers and 75 percent of fathers said it was "very true" that there is always something more to learn as parent. Parents who say they can always learn something more about parenting say that they:

- are willing to tap into a variety of sources that have support and information;
- more often seek out the support of family, friends, and community resources;
- less often feel overwhelmed or unprepared as parents; and
- parent their children in more ways that help their children grow up well.

How Your Congregation Can Help Parents Feel Less Isolated

As a congregation, you have much to offer parents so they feel less alone. How can you do this when you already have

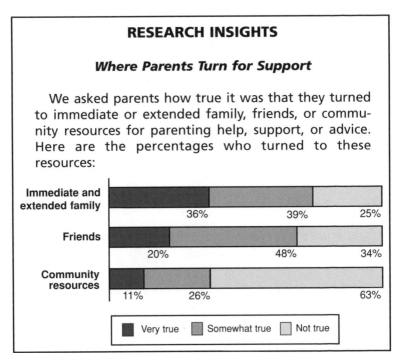

RESEARCH INSIGHTS

Where Parents Turn for Support

We asked parents how true it was that they turned to immediate or extended family, friends, or community resources for parenting help, support, or advice. Here are the percentages who turned to these resources:

Immediate and extended family: 36% 39% 25%

Friends: 20% 48% 34%

Community resources: 11% 26% 63%

Legend: ■ Very true ■ Somewhat true □ Not true

a full plate with many needs? Start thinking big by starting small in significant ways. Supporting parents doesn't have to entail starting a new ministry or even a new program. Consider some of these ideas:

• *Create an environment where help-seeking and mutual support are honored*—Too often in our society, seeking help and support from others is perceived as a sign of weakness or inadequacy, especially among men. So it's little wonder that many parents, particularly fathers, seem to be reluctant to seek help from others. What will people think? Will they assume they are bad parents if they admit they're struggling or facing a challenge?

Congregations can remind parents and others that we are created to need and rely on each other. Seeking help and support is a sign of health and a key to successful parenting. Use sermons, bulletins, educational events, and other communication opportunities to reinforce this perspective. Model a sense of vulnerability and help seeking. Equip people within your congregation and your community with knowledge and skills to be positive, trustworthy resources when parents seek help.

• *Incorporate a parent gathering into an educational or fellowship activity*—Once a year (or maybe a number of times a year), invite all the parents to their children's Christian education class. (Have the entire class be a family-friendly class.) Have one leader do activities with the parents that help parents get to know each other while another leader does activities with the children. End the class with an activity that parents and children can do together. If you have many parents who have more than one child, invite parents to only one grade (or age grouping) per week so that parents don't feel pulled between attending different classes. Also consider doing this for a youth group gathering, a confirmation class, or other activities that are designed for young people in your congregation. It's one thing to build community among the children and youth; it's another to build it among their parents.

• *Create a parent education class*—Many congregations have an adult education class. Those that have these classes

21

A CONGREGATION SUCCESS STORY

Helping Single Parents Not Feel Alone

Single parents, who may feel overwhelmed with the challenges of parenting alone and providing everything their children need, can find connection, support, and opportunities to grow at Second Baptist Church in Houston, Texas. Through its Single Plus ministry, single parents come together to meet other single parents.

The congregation offers an annual Single Parent Family Vacation. Each summer, single-parent families take a vacation together through the congregation. The group has vacationed in cabins in the Rocky Mountains of Colorado; chateaus in Branson, Missouri; lodges in Arkansas; the Flying L Guest Ranch in Bandera, Texas; and the Opryland Hotel in Nashville.

During the year, the congregation offers a Second Gear program that provides automobile maintenance and repair for single parents. Second Gear is open Monday through Friday from 9:00 A.M. to 5:00 P.M., and single parents are charged only for parts and materials, not for labor. The congregation creates a volunteer bank of mechanics that provide all the automotive work.

often lament that the people who attend are typically older members. Start an additional class that's designed just for parents. Most publishers of Christian adult education curriculum have workbooks, leader guides, and classes for parents.

• *Develop supports for all kinds of parents*—Many congregations have a parent support group that meets during the day for stay-at-home parents, but then working parents get missed. At Church Street United Methodist Church in Knoxville, Tennessee, parents can choose from two different support groups: one that meets on Wednesday mornings at 9:30 or one that meets on Sunday evenings at 6. The Sunday evening group meets at the same time children attend the congregation's Sunday evening activities.

• *Create visible roles for parents in your congregation*—Many congregations have countless opportunities for parents

22

to get involved, but these activities tend to be hidden away from the rest of the congregation. Parents may be volunteering in the nursery or in a Christian education class. Recruit parents to be ushers, liturgists, worship assistants, musicians, and other visible roles during worship. Outside of worship, work to include parents on your leadership team and other important committees, not just the committees that revolve around children, youth, and families.

• *Expand your concept of congregational care*—Whether your congregation calls this *pastoral care* or *congregational care*, expect all members of the congregation to minister to each other. In many congregations this care often turns into only crisis care. It's about visiting the sick, the hospitalized, and the homebound. It's about praying for those who are in dire need.

The truth is, we all need care. Effective congregations often create circles of care where every regular church attending person (member or not) is assigned to a "care group." Sometimes these are by geographic location (according to where these people live) or by interest, such as a parenting teens group, a young adult group, a seniors group, and so on. Consider ways that all members can be included in receiving and giving care.

A number of congregations also have expanded their idea of congregational care to mark the major transitions of parenting. Some congregations hold a baby shower for each expectant parent. (Or if the congregation is large, they have a small group that does this.) Other congregations cook a meal for the first day (or even first week) that a family comes home with a baby from the hospital or an adopted baby arrives.

Identify the major changes that parents go through and figure out ways to care for parents during these times. Obviously pregnancy (or the completion of a homestudy) and the arrival of a child are some of the first major changes. But what about marking the transition of a child going to kindergarten for the first time? Sometimes the parents are more anxious than the child is. Or what about when a child

RESEARCH INSIGHTS

How Many Sources of Support Do Parents Tap?

Parents were offered three potential sources of support that they might turn to: (1) immediate or extended family, (2) friends, and (3) community resources. We then calculated the proportion of parents who regularly sought support from these potential parenting resources.* We also discovered that parents who attend a congregation weekly or more are much more likely to turn to these supports compared to parents who rarely or never go to a congregation.

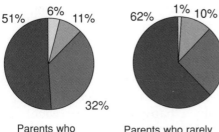

Parents who attend religious services weekly or more

Parents who rarely attend religious services services

*These figures are based on parents who said it was "very true" that they turned to each group for parenting help, advice, or support.

■ None
■ One of three
□ Two of three
□ Three of three

turns 13? Parents often joke about becoming the parent of a teenager, but it often is a time that raises parental concern. High school graduation is another one, as is a child leaving for college for the first time.

Congregations that have a number of families with college-age students sometimes create a care basket for the first-time parent of a college-bound student. Others have created parent support groups to help parents adjust to this new type of parenting from afar. Still others have created e-mails (or letter-writing campaigns) to help college students feel more connected to their parents and the congregation.

• *Give parents concrete and safe opportunities to ask for support*— Recently, laypeople at Aldersgate United Methodist Church in St. Louis Park, Minnesota, were conducting a survey of all congregational members. As they went through the church directory to see who had and hadn't completed the survey, they noted several members they didn't think had the energy to participate because of the struggles they were facing in their families. However, instead of leaving these people alone ("not bothering them"), team members agreed that they should use the opportunity to check in with all families, let them know their opinions were valued, and offer support and encouragement, if it was needed. In the process, the team opened up opportunities for parents to share their concerns without having to take all the initiative.

• *Create opportunities for people to talk to each other*—In many committee meetings and other activities of the congregation, the first and last order of business tends to be business. Develop an intentional time in each

A CONGREGATION SUCCESS STORY

Connecting Parents Who Homeschool Their Children

With the homeschooling movement growing, many congregations recognize that it's easy for parents to become even more isolated as a stay-at-home parent if the parent also is taking on the responsibility of homeschooling the children. At Saddleback Church in Lake Forest, California, congregational leaders have created an extensive homeschooling ministry to help parents connect with each other and to encourage a high-quality education for children who are homeschooled.

The congregation offers a monthly newsletter on the subject, a roster of homeschooling families, and a monthly networking event. To enhance the learning process, the congregation provides monthly field trips, a community service project, school photos, educational testing assistance, a study hall for homeschoolers age 6 and older, a lending library of books and tapes, and monthly assemblies.

For parents who have just decided to start homeschooling, the congregation gives informational meetings along with a resource list to get started.

committee meeting, congregation activity, and educational class for people to have a short time to talk with each other. Create a short conversation starter where everyone talks and listens. For example, include a get-to-know-you question in a meeting, activity, or class. These questions could be: What do you love doing in your spare time? Who do you look up to most and why? How do you spend most of your day Monday through Friday? What is your favorite TV show? Where did you grow up? How many people live with you and who are they? Ask questions that encourage people to reveal something about themselves in nonthreatening ways. As people talk and listen, they'll begin to make more connections with one another.

• *Provide meaningful service for families to do together*— Some people like to connect by talking with others. But that may be threatening or uncomfortable for others. Or they may not see it as a "productive" priority. Engaging families in leadership and service that is meaningful *to them* can be a great vehicle for support and relationship building for parents. By working together to accomplish shared goals, such as organizing an event or serving together in a soup kitchen, family members (parents and children) grow closer to one another and to other families. In addition, these hands-on projects can be excellent opportunities for forming intergenerational relationships that benefit everyone.

• *Designate someone to get to know parents*—This may be a lay leader or a congregational staff person, but having one person in charge can transform your congregation into a more parent-friendly congregation. All this person needs to do is to seek out the parents in your congregation and talk with them briefly. Get to know their names. Find out how they spend their day. Learn what their joys and concerns are. Then connect parents with others who have similar interests and concerns. This is how some congregations discover that they have a group of parents who have adopted (and then create an activity for this group) or a group of parents seeking family service projects. If you don't know the parents, how can they know each other?

• *Create a parent directory*—When registering teens for Christian education or for youth activities, have a form that also asks for information about the parents. What are the parents' first and last names? Where do they live? What is their phone number? What age (or grade level) of children do they have? Have a checkbox on the form stating that the parents give permission for their names to be included in a directory. Then create a parent directory for your entire congregation (particularly if you have a small congregation) or a directory for each grade level (or age grouping) of children.

• *Ask for parents' input*—Find a time to have parents meet and give their input for making your congregation a better place for them. Some congregations call these focus groups, others make them into gatherings where parents get to know one another and give feedback. You'll get the most helpful input if you can ask parents specific questions. You may even want to conduct a written survey of parents. See the box "Questions to Ask Parents" on page 28 for ideas.

Connecting Parents to One Another—and to Your Congregation

Parents and families are more likely to come to a congregation when they feel connected to your community of faith. They also will attend more often. That's good for them, and that's good for your congregation.

You can help parents feel less alone. Connect them to each other. Include them in your congregational community so that they feel like valued members. Create an atmosphere of genuine care that everyone can feel and experience. Do this through your worship services, your educational opportunities, your committee meetings, your fellowship time. Weave this deep sense of care in whatever you do, and parents will see what a valuable place your congregation is.

Questions to Ask Parents

You can minister more effectively to parents if you seek them out and ask them questions. Whether you talk with parents individually or have them meet as a group, ask detailed questions, such as these:

- Why do you come to our congregation?
- How many people do you know at this congregation who are also parents?
- What do you like best about being a parent? Why?
- How could our congregation better support you as a parent?
- What does our congregation do best for parents?
- What is your biggest challenge as a parent?
- Where are parents most visible in our congregation?
- Where are parents least visible in our congregation?
- How well does our congregation help your family grow in faith?
- What do you wish our congregation offered to make your life easier as a parent?
- Who are the people in your congregation whom you feel comfortable approaching if you are facing challenges as a parent? If you don't have anyone in mind, what qualities would you look for in such a person?

Chapter 2

Finding #2: Many Parents Lack a Strong Relationship with a Spouse or Partner

*W*HAT HELPS PARENTS succeed? People often point to income, education, or race. Yet we found that the *quality* of the parents' relationship (whether or not they were married) proved to be the most important factor in raising children well. This was even more important than income, education, profession, religion, and race.[1] Parents in this poll who reported having an excellent relationship with their partner were more likely to feel successful and up to the challenges of parenting. These parents even had significant advantages over the parents who rated their relationship as good.

Why Parents Need a Strong Partner

Countless studies have found that a high-quality relationship with a spouse or partner is a powerful resource for parenting success. Researchers have discovered direct links between the quality of the parents' relationship and how well children developed. The better the parents' relationship, the more likely children grew up well.[2]

This is true whether or not parents are married. Although research has shown that children benefit when they have contact with a noncustodial parents, other studies point out that children actually suffer if the parents have severe conflicts with each other.[3]

What matters is the amount of conflict between parents. Even married parents who have a lot of conflict can inflict a lot of pain and damage onto their children. Researcher John Gottman has written extensively about how parents can work through their conflicts and develop relationships that are more nurturing between parents and also between parents and children.[4]

Besides being beneficial to the kids, researchers also have found that a strong relationship between partners is helpful to the adults involved. Researcher Linda Waite even concluded that married people are happier, healthier, and better off financially. She says that husbands and wives who were quite unhappy with their marriage but stuck with it and

A CONGREGATION SUCCESS STORY

Enriching Marriages in Many Ways

Congregational leaders at East Hill Church in Gresham, Oregon, believe "a strong marriage is the starting point for a healthy family." Because of this belief, the congregation offers classes, support groups, renewal weekends, and marriage celebrations to strengthen the marriages of members.

Every spring, the congregation offers a romantic weekend for couples to focus on their marriage. Couples not only learn how to connect more deeply but also learn practical skills to improve their relationship.

The congregation offers three different classes: an eight-week class for couples married five years or less, a 10-week class for couples interested in refreshing their love life, and an eight-week class on building more intimate relationships through communication and conflict resolution. Couples who have completed the eight-week class on building more intimate relationships can join a marriage support group.

Each November, the congregation holds a marriage celebration. Couples renew their vows and also find out new ways to renew some fun in their relationship.

worked through their unhappiness went on to have much happier marriages later. People in congregations have long argued about the importance of marriage and why it's good for children; Waite's study is part of a growing research base that makes the scientific case for marriage.[5]

In polling parents, we found that a strong relationship between parents was beneficial to the parents and the children. Of the parents we polled, those who reported an excellent relationship with their spouse or partner were more likely than other parents to:

- experience fewer challenges as parents;
- feel confident in dealing with the daily challenges of parenting;
- seek support from immediate or extended family as well as community resources;
- feel successful as parents most of the time;
- believe that certain opportunities (such as talking with other parents or seeking advice from a trusted professional) could really help them as parents; and
- engage in parenting strategies that contribute to the healthy development of their children.

How Parents Rate Their Partner

Despite the importance of a high-quality relationship between parents, only half of those surveyed rate their relationship with their spouse or partner as excellent. Twelve percent said their relationship was fair to poor.

Although married parents were more likely to report having an excellent relationship with their spouse, marriage itself does not guarantee a high-quality relationship (though it makes one much more likely). Among married parents, 56 percent said they have an excellent relationship; 36 percent of unmarried parents say the same about their parenting partner.

RESEARCH INSIGHTS

Quality of Parent Partnerships

We asked parents to describe their relationship with their current spouse or partner. Here's how parents rated their partner:

7%

12%

Excellent
Good
Okay to poor
Does not apply

31%

50%

Isn't a good relationship good enough? We found that good was better than fair to poor, but a good relationship didn't produce the benefits that an excellent relationship did. Analysis of the data revealed that parents tended to feel consistently more successful (and actually were in some cases) when they had an excellent relationship instead of just a good relationship with their partner.

"The research consensus is that a 'healthy marriage'—and not just any marriage—is optimal for child well-being," conclude researchers at Child Trends, a research center dedicated to improving the lives of children and families. "Research clearly demonstrates that family structures matter for children, and the family structure that helps children the most is a family headed by two biological parents in a low-conflict marriage."[6]

Some people may react to this research as being judgmental against single parents and those with a difficult marriage or partner relationship. It's important to be clear: A strong relationship between parents—particularly a strong marriage—is better for children and for parents. As a result, congregations and other institutions that care about young people's healthy growth and development do well to support and encourage strong marriages. However, for many different reasons, many parents do not have the benefit of that kind of relationship. That's not a reason to blame or shame those parents. Rather, congregations and others need to do whatever they can to offer compensating supports that help to provide a web of care and positive relationships for both the parents and the children.

Parents in Religious Families

Parents in religious families treat each other differently from parents who never do anything religious. According to other research, young people who say their families do something religious five to seven days a week (such as go to church, pray, or read scripture together) say their parents are more affectionate toward each other. Seventy-one percent of young people living in religious families say their mothers always express affection or love to their fathers, whereas only 46 percent of young people living in families who never do anything religious say this is true.[7]

Young people also witnessed their fathers being more affectionate toward their mothers when they lived in religious families. Sixty-nine percent of young people who live in religious families say their fathers express affection or love to their mothers compared to only 45 percent of young people who live in families that never do anything religious.[8]

Every day of religious activity makes a difference in the way married parents interact with each other. Fifty-two percent of young people who live in families that do something religious only one or two days a week say their mom expresses affection toward their father. That percentage jumps to 63 percent for young people who live in families that do something religious three to four days a week. These findings are true not only for mothers but also for fathers.[9]

How Your Congregation Can Nurture Partner Relationships

Nurturing adults in two-parent families is one thing and ministering to single parents is another. Your congregation can do both, and you'll often be more effective if you create separate strategies for these two types of parents. Before you begin, consider these suggestions:

RESEARCH INSIGHTS

Married Parents Go to Church More

Although 69 percent of parents in the United States are living in two-parent families (with 31 percent being single parents),[10] congregations are more likely to see married parents come to church than unmarried couples. Congregations also are more likely to see married parents much more involved in the congregation, attending more often. According to the poll of 1,005 parents surveyed by Search Institute, the following chart shows how often parents attend church according to their marital status:

	Attend church weekly or more	Attend church less than weekly but at least once a month	Attend church every few months	Rarely or never attend church
Married Parents	64%	14%	7%	15%
Unmarried Parents	52%	15%	9%	24%

• *Work to define what family is*—How does your congregation define family? Which types of families are you willing to minister to? Nurturing a relationship between two adults who live and parent together requires some theological and programmatic thinking on your congregation's part since some people have strong feelings about certain types of families. Controversy can arise within your congregation when two-parent families are made up of unmarried couples or same-sex couples. Although there are types of single-parent families that can also stir up your congregational gossip lines (such as an unmarried mother who had her first child as a teenager or a gay parent who adopts), single parents often can hide these things easier than two same-sex parents arriving at your worship service with children. If your congregation is not welcoming to all types of families, the ones that feel judged will stay away. Or if some members and leaders in your congregation are open while others are not, you'll soon find people at odds with each other.

Some congregations have developed a process to work with members to develop an open and affirming stance toward all types of families. Others have had congregational leaders take a stand on the types of ministries they'll offer—and why. Diana Garland, the editor of *Family Ministry* journal and director of the Center for Family and Community Ministries at Baylor University recommends that congregations shift from defining family as a married couple and their children (if they have any) to defining family as the persons who commit themselves to attempt to be family for one another.[11]

• *Affirm and celebrate relationships*—Figure out easy ways to celebrate relationships between couples. Some congregations host a Valentine's sweetheart dinner. Others have an annual relationship celebration. Some even encourage couples to go on overnight getaways through congregational camps or other programs. One organization is Marriage Encounter, which works to build deep and loving communication between a husband, a wife, and God. Many denominations

Marriage Encounter Contacts

A number of congregations encourage married couples to attend Marriage Encounter retreats and conferences to enhance the quality of their marriage. These retreats typically occur over a weekend where couples renew their relationships by focusing on the way they communicate with each other. Many denominations have worked with Marriage Encounter to infuse the model with the specific beliefs and practices of their denomination. For more information, contact these denominations or http://www.marriage-encounter.org:

- Baptist Marriage Encounter—
  http://www.wcrtc.com/~dlott/beofme
- Catholic Marriage Encounter—
  http://www.wwme.org
- Disciples of Christ Marriage Encounter—
  http://home.pacbell.net/wolcottp/links.htm
- Episcopal Marriage Encounter—
  http://www.episcopalme.com
- Lutheran Marriage Encounter—
  http://www.ilme.org
- Mennonite and Brethren Marriage Encounter—
  http://www.marriageenounter.org
- Presbyterian Marriage Encounter—
  http://www.presby-me.org
- United Church of Christ Marriage Encounter—
  http://home.pacbell.net/wolcottp/links.htm
- United Methodist Marriage Encounter—
  http://www.encounter.org
- Other Denominations and the National Marriage Encounter—http://www.marriage-encounter.org.

have affiliations with Marriage Encounter. See the box "Marriage Encounter Contacts."

• *Create occasional couple events*—Couples find certain congregational events more appealing than others. Researchers who interviewed 947 couples involved in congregations found that they would most likely use child care at congregational events, follow-up to marriage preparation, new-parent get togethers, parenting workshops, pregnancy classes, a monthly congregation service for couples, educational classes about the congregation, and refresher marriage courses.[12]

Consider creating a monthly religious education class for parents where they get together to talk about essential relationship topics. Or create a couple's night out where you offer child care while couples come together and talk about their relationship. Have couples write love letters to each other (which is something that tends to fall by the wayside once children show up) or talk about their couple rituals (such as talking in bed each night, always kissing before they go off to work, or cooking dinner once a week). Another interesting activity is having couples figure out how many days they've been together. (Remind them to include the extra day for leap year.) Then encourage them to celebrate their relationship on the next big day, such as day one thousand, two thousand, five thousand, ten thousand.

• *Help parents enhance their parenting partnerships*— Consider offering classes, workshops, or gatherings that affirm the partnerships that parents have with each other. Teach parents how to process and work through issues that may be hindering their relationship or just keeping it flat and distant. One survey found that money tops parents' list of concerns with communication, money for college, time management, and time with family as other concerns.[13] Another research study discovered that premarital couples who attend courses that focus on their relationship tend to communicate better, solve problems, and report better relationships than couples who do not participate in such programs.[14]

A Congregation Success Story

A Marriage Conference at the Church

Couples at First Baptist Church in Nashville attended a covenant marriage conference at their congregation that was provided for a small fee. The conference began on a Friday night with a candlelight dinner followed by a session on how to move from marriage contracts to marriage covenants.

In the morning, couples returned to learn about effective communication and how to celebrate the "activity of God in your marriage." The cost ($25 per couple) made it easy for parents to attend, and the cost included child care.

A number of ministers have been trained in the Prepare/Enrich program. This program helps couples get ready for marriage (through the Prepare program) and then enhances the relationship of those who are already married (through the Enrich program). Clergy only need to attend a one-day workshop to be trained, and trainers will even set up this workshop at your congregation if you don't have a workshop near you. Developed by David H. Olson, Ph.D., this program has been building stronger relationship for more than 20 years. Even if you don't become trained, you can link up with trained clergy by visiting the Web site for names or trained clergy near you at www.lifeinnovation.com.

• *Don't assume that family life works just because a family has two parents*—Although it's preferable that kids have two parents instead of one, two-parent families sometimes don't work as well as they appear. One out of five women is a victim of intimate partner violence every year. The most common type of violence is simple assault, which includes threats, attacks without weapons, and attempted attacks.[15] Of women who are killed each year, one out of three is killed by a spouse, a partner, or a boyfriend.[16] Although these statistics highlight some of the worst things that can happen in families, there are also families where relationships are strained. Some families are struggling with issues that congregations avoid or gloss over. Pay attention to these dynamics and make your congregation a safe place where people can be open with their struggles. Ensure that you know appropriate ways to respond and refer if issues of abuse or neglect become evident.

• *Tap into the opportunities from marriage enrichment—* Many congregations use the training and expertise of Marriage Enrichment, an association that promotes better marriages through enrichment opportunities. Because people from this organization have been conducting workshops, trainings, and other marriage enrichment events for congregations since the 1960s, they know much about how to attract and keep couples coming. Contact: The Association for Couples in Marriage Enrichment, P.O. Box 10596, Winston-Salem, NC 27108; 800-634-8325; fax: 336-721-4746; www.bettermarriages.org.

• *Consider linking new couples with older couples*—Some congregations create couple mentoring programs, and these can be effective if couples see them as advantageous and if your congregation links all couples with each other, instead of just a few. One study found that only 5 percent of young couples had used these mentoring programs, and less than one third said they would consider this

A CONGREGATION SUCCESS STORY

Giving a Voice to Married Parents

Married couples can join marriage groups through the Crossroads Church of Denver. These groups, which meet in people's homes throughout the Denver metropolitan area, encourage couples to share their personal experiences and connect with one another. The groups also focus on a specific topic each time, and topics have included:

• The Five Love Languages
• Growing Together in Christ
• Improving Communication in Your Marriage
• How to Manage Your Money
• Loving Your Spouse

39

type of program.[17] This idea may be more appealing if it is more informal and designed to help couples get to know other couples in your congregation.

• *Create marriage study groups*—Certified marriage enrichment leaders Preston Dyer and Genie Dyer recommend two books for couples to study in small groups. One is *The Lasting Promise: A Christian Guide to Fighting for Your Marriage* by Scott Stanley, Daniel Trathen, Savanna McCain, and Milt Bryan (published by Jossey Bass, San Francisco, 1998). The other is *The Seven Principles for Making Marriages Work* by John Gottman and Nan Silver (published by Crown Publishers, New York, 1999).[18]

• *Collect and recognize anniversary dates*—Some congregations find out the birthdays of each member and publish them in the bulletin or congregation newsletter. Consider also collecting anniversary dates of couples and recognize these dates. If you also have couples who aren't officially married, ask them for the date that they mark as the beginning of their relationship. Consider presenting some type of meaningful token, such as a single-stem rose during a worship service to mark the anniversary of a couple. If you do this for everyone (and not just on the silver and golden anniversaries), your congregation shows how much it values long-term relationships and the commitments couples make to keep them going.

When Parents Don't Have a Partner

Although some single parents have joint custody or some type of relationship with their former spouse, a number of single parents don't have much or any contact with their child's other parent. One of five single parents doesn't receive child support because the other parent cannot be located.[19]

Even without the involvement of the other parent, these single parents do not have to go it alone. Your congregation can help them find other supports and even identify another adult (or a number of adults) who would be willing to take on important roles in the family.

One mother who had adopted a child from Peru wanted her son to have a male adult role model. Through her congregation, she found a man in his 60s who took a liking to her son and agreed to do special activities with her son periodically. He took the preschool-age boy to the circus and to the park. The man and the boy got together four to six times a year, and doing so consistently helped to form a bond between the two of them.

Much research points to the disadvantages that kids have when they live in single-parent homes. They're more likely to live in poverty, be isolated from others, and are more likely to be victimized.[20] On the average, kids do better when they live in two-parent families. Yet, researchers point out that some young people (though not as many) also do well in single-parent families.[21] This is the research that congregational leaders can tap into and use to minister to single-parent families effectively.

Part of the strategy is to build developmental assets, which are the key building blocks that young people need to succeed.[22] Search Institute researchers have found that young people who live in single-parent families are more likely to thrive when they experience more of these assets in their lives.[23] Much of the difference between young people in single-parent families who thrive and those who don't revolves around the support systems that surround families. This is where your congregation can make a significant difference. Young people who live in single-parent families are more likely to succeed when they're involved in religious institutions, supportive schools, meaningful extracurricular activities, and have friends who influence them in positive ways. "It may be that this external network of support is key to success in single parenting," conclude the researchers.[24]

If a congregation can make a difference by building developmental assets in young people who live in single-parent families and by providing support to these families, what else can they do to help single parents succeed?

• *Seek out single parents and their children*—If you did only one thing in your congregation, the one thing that would make a large difference would be getting to know single parents and their children. Learn their names. Talk with them. Connect them with other people in your congregation who sincerely and genuinely care about them. When they come, go out of your way to call them by name and welcome them. Creating a warm, open, and inviting atmosphere toward single-parent families helps them feel wanted and encourages them to come back. When congregations make a special effort, they can help single parents and their children feel welcome and important.

• *Teach single parents healthy parenting skills*—"The quality of a mother-child relationship is the single most critical factor in determining how children feel about themselves in the postdivorce decade and how well they function in the various domains in their lives," write researchers Judith S. Wallerstein and Sandra Blakeslee.[25] When you provide educational opportunities for parents, don't single out single parents. Create classes and workshops that teach these essential skills to all parents. Then work to ensure that single parents come. This isn't an easy task since there are many barriers that keep single parents from getting the help they need. If they need transportation, offer it. If they don't want to make another trip to your congregation, have the class before or after a worship service when their children are involved in religious education or another congregational activity. Team up with parent educators in the congregation or community to teach these parenting skills. Parents and children often see their relationships improve when they learn how to communicate more effectively, listen to each other more, resolve conflicts peacefully, set and enforce respectful boundaries, and find activities that they enjoy doing together.

• *Emphasize the importance of parent relationships on children*—Even for divorced or separated parents, the relationship does not end just because their marriage has. Help single parents identify the quality of their relationship with their former spouse, particularly if they have some contact with that person or he or she periodically sees the children. In North Carolina, the Family Life Council of Greater Greensboro provides a program for parenting children of divorce. Surveying parents about two months after completing the program, program providers have found that three of four parents say that they had gained information to improve things with their former spouse and had a less acrimonious relationship.[26]

Sometimes parents will not get help, and former spouses verbally abuse each other and their kids. Because leaders saw a number of children in their community have stressful custodial exchanges, the Visalia YMCA in California set up the Safe Exchange Program to provide a safe, neutral environment for court-ordered exchanges between custodial parents. When an exchange needs to occur, the one parent drops off the child at the center. Children then stay at the center for up to an hour before the other parent arrives to pick them up. (Those who designed this program worked to ensure that parents with contentious relationships would not be at the center at the same time.) Over time, children and the parents become less stressed. As stress levels drop, staff members then help parents to work on their relationship with each other. One young couple created a written agreement establishing goals so that they as parents could eventually do exchanges at home. "We help parents put their children first," says Safe Exchange Coordinator Kris McClure. "This type of program helps everyone—the parents and the kids."[27]

• *Focus on the economic hardship*—One of the biggest obstacles for many single parents is poverty. Half of all single mothers live below the poverty line compared to only 10 percent of two-parent families. Talk with single parents and find out about the involvement of the other parent, if there is one. See if there's anything you can do regarding child support. Many single parents have been rewarded child support but haven't received any money. Of those who actually receive payments, single mothers receive only 60 percent of the amount promised while fathers receive only 48 percent.[28] One single mother (who had been working two jobs and was completely stressed out) didn't receive any child support until another adult offered to help. After talking with the former husband, the adult discovered that he couldn't afford to pay the full child-support amount. The two negotiated until a new payment plan was made that was for half the amount. Even though it wasn't as much as the courts had awarded this single mother, the truth was that she wasn't receiving any payments. Receiving half the amount was enough to allow her to quit one of her jobs and to be able to focus more on her family and taking care of herself.

Some congregations have set up college scholarships for young people in single-parent homes. Others have provided other services, such as finding (and subsidizing) after-school child care, providing meaningful activities for children who live in single-parent families (along with the transportation), and connecting single parents with resources in the community that have been set up to support single parents.

Others have simply encouraged single parents to connect with each other. For example, four single-parent families got together and formed a weekly support team. One parent cared for all the other children while the other three parents either went out or worked together to help another one of the parents, such as doing a thorough cleaning of the home, painting a room, or setting up for a teen's confirmation party.

How to Build Strong Partner Relationships

There is clear evidence that children and teenagers benefit from a strong partner relationship. Although most of the scientific literature focuses on what makes marriages unhealthy (such as criticism, contempt, and stonewalling), the research of John Gottman has finally focused on how to make relationships work.

Gottman has identified seven principles to making a marriage work. These principles include how to nurture fondness and how to overcome gridlock. "In the strongest marriages, husband and wife share a deep sense of meaning," he says. "They don't just 'get along'—they also support each other's hopes and aspirations and build a sense of purpose into their lives together."[29]

David and Vera Mace, leading thinkers and advocates for strong Christian marriages, have published many books on effective marriages. Their book, *In the Presence of God: Readings for Christian Marriage,* is a best-seller that includes thought-provoking readings, biblical references, quotations, reflections, and prayers.

Success in Marriage, the classic book written by David Mace in 1958, gives practical advice on how to make marriages rich and satisfying. His book *Close Companions: The Marriage Enrichment Handbook* is considered the handbook on marriage for congregational leaders interested in nurturing relationships between couples.

In whatever ways you support couples, help them see how their relationship affects their parenting. As couples nurture their relationship, not only will they become more satisfied with their relationship but they also will become more effective parents. Parents need energy and time to focus on the kids, and they're more apt to have that time and energy when their partner relationships are going well.

Chapter 3

Finding #3: Many Parents Feel Successful as Parents Most of the Time

*A*LTHOUGH THE media likes to portray parents at their worst and our society likes to judge parents harshly in general, researchers have found that most parents are doing a reasonably good job as parents. While there are no perfect parents and there are some parents who hurt their children extensively through abuse or neglect, most parents meet their children's basic needs and help them grow up well.

Not only is it important how parents are doing but also how parents feel about their parenting. While there are slight differences among parents surveyed, we found that most parents feel successful as parents most of the time.

How Parents Define Parenting Success

How do parents define parenting success? We asked parents directly, and we got a wide range of answers. The top four definitions that rose from the data included:

- having children who are respectful, exhibit good behavior, and have positive values;
- giving love to their children;
- being involved and making time to be there for their children; and

• helping their children lead a healthy, productive, successful life.

What we also found is that parents tended to define success in the positive rather than the negative ways. Only 1 percent of parents surveyed said that the definition of a successful parent was keeping their children off drugs. Most pointed to raising their children in ways that helped their children develop well and succeed.

How Often Parents Feel Successful

Most parents surveyed say they feel successful as parents most of the time. About one third say they feel successful as parents nearly every day. Fifty-four percent say they feel successful on most days. Some differences exist among parents about how successful they feel. The following groups of parents are more likely than others to feel successful:

• younger parents (those age 18 to 34);
• parents who have lived in their neighborhood from one to five years;
• parents whose child is 4 years old or younger, particularly compared to parents of 11- to 15-year-olds;
• parents who have an excellent relationship with their spouse or partner; and
• African American parents compared to white parents.

What do these results mean? First, the age of the child, the age of the parents, and the length of time in a neighborhood may suggest that parents may feel more successful in the earlier stages of parenting rather than the later.

How parents "feel" about their parenting and how they're actually "doing" as parents are actually two different things. Most parents tend to become even more effective when they feel they're on the right track, but it's also true that some parents have misperceptions about themselves. Congregations can give parents concrete ways to help parents feel like they're succeeding when they actually are. The developmental asset framework is one proven strategy that makes parenting practical. Chapter 6 presents the asset framework and explores various ways to present it to parents in your congregation.

A CONGREGATION SUCCESS STORY

Helping Parents Succeed with Everyday Issues

Parents at Bell Shoals Baptist Church in Brandon, Florida, don't need to be in crisis or have trouble to participate in a ministry for parents. The congregation offers classes, encouragement groups (instead of support groups), special events, weekly Bible studies, and a "Mom's Place" for moms to get together once a month.

Through these different opportunities, parents learn about how to be more effective on a daily basis. Topics include managing your time, enhancing your marriage, creating a compassionate home, developing financial peace, shattering the "superwoman" myth, and recognizing the important relationships in your life.

At Mom's Place, the congregation creates topics that appeal to all moms who are parenting children of different ages. To make it easier for moms who have young children, the congregation offers child care during Mom's Place.

Which Parenting Tasks Parents Do Well

Parents included in the poll were also asked about a number of ways they contribute to their children's healthy development. The items were based on Search Institute's research-based framework of the 40 developmental assets. The 11 parenting actions related to each of the eight categories of assets. (See the box "Parenting Actions and Developmental Assets" on pages 50-51.)

RESEARCH INSIGHTS

Parenting Actions and Developmental Assets

Parents were asked about how often they do the following 11 specific parenting actions. Each of the parenting actions relates to one of the eight categories of assets. The 11 parenting actions encompass the entire asset framework with at least one question covering one of the categories of assets.

Parenting Action	Category of Asset
• Show love and affection for your child. (See asset #1: family support.) • Encourage other adults you trust to spend positive time with your child. (See asset #3: other adult relationships.)	Support Assets (Assets #1-#6)
• Encourage your child to help other people, including volunteering in his or her school, congregation, club, or community. (See asset #9: service to others.)	Empowerment Assets (Assets #7-#10)
• Get to know your child's friends. (See asset #15: positive peer influence.)	Boundaries & Expectations Assets (Assets #11-#16)
• Ensure your child participates in arts, sports, recreation, or educational programs or activities outside of school. (See asset #17: creative activities and asset #18: youth programs.) • Ensure your child is active in a church, synagogue, mosque, or other religious organization. (See asset #19: religious community.)	Constructive Use of Time Assets (Assets #17-#20)

Parenting Action	Category of Asset
• Help your child enjoy learning new things or working hard at schoolwork. (See asset #21: achievement motivation and asset #22: school engagement.)	Commitment to Learning Assets (Assets #21-#25)
• Teach your child basic values such as equality, honesty, and responsibility. (See asset #27: equality and social justice, asset #29: honesty, and #30: responsibility.)	Positive Values Assets (Assets #26-#31)
• Teach your child a social skill such as how to understand the feelings of others. (See asset #33: interpersonal competence.) • Teach your child to get along well with people of different races and backgrounds. (See asset #34: cultural competence.)	Social Competencies Assets (Assets #32-#36)
• Help your child feel he or she is good at doing something. (See asset #38: self-esteem.)	Positive Identity Assets (Assets #37-#40)

When asked about how often parents do these 11 selected parenting actions, at least three fourths of the parents surveyed do all of these things at least weekly. Some even do them daily. Across all incomes, racial and cultural groups, educational levels, and types of families in this poll, most of the parents surveyed report that they regularly do things to ensure that their children have what they need to grow up caring and competent.

While the differences among these 11 parenting actions are not dramatic, they do suggest that parents are more likely to focus on what they can do themselves for their children rather than connecting with people and places that can contribute to their children's healthy development.

We found that parents are most likely to do the parenting actions that can be completed through one-to-one relationships with their children. The top five actions that nine out of 10 of these parents do at least weekly can occur within the family. The remaining six actions require that parents connect with others in the community.

One of the least common actions involves parents encouraging other adults to spend time with their child. In chapter 5, parents reveal in Finding #5 that one of the most helpful things for parents would be "people I trust, such as friends, neighbors, or extended family spending a greater amount of time with my child." Other Search Institute research shows that a major barrier to other adults' active engagement with children who aren't their own is a perceived lack of parental permission or invitation to be involved.[1]

How Your Congregation Can Help Parents Feel Successful

Parenting is one of those jobs where there is no annual review and no outside assessment of how parents are doing (unless the state's Child Protection Services is considering removing a child from the home due to abuse or neglect). Parents aren't required to take any training or learn any skills. (Although prospective adoptive parents often feel they are carefully scrutinized.) This is where congregations can have a major impact on helping parents by supporting parents and helping them feel successful. Consider some of these ideas:

• *Teach parents the developmental asset framework to help them and their children succeed*—Many congregations now use the developmental asset framework in their family ministry, children's ministry, youth ministry, and religious education. Some even use the framework as a lens for everything the congregation does. Once parents see how developmental assets protect their kids from dangerous behaviors, promote positive behaviors, and help them bounce back from difficult situations, they're often inspired to use the framework in their parenting. See

RESEARCH INSIGHTS

How Often Parents Feel Successful

We asked 1,005 parents how often they feel successful as parents. Here is what they said:

12%

34%

54%

- ■ Nearly every day
- ■ Most days
- ☐ About half the time or less

chapters 6 and 7 for more specifics on how to teach parents the asset framework and how to use the asset framework to transform your congregation.

- *Check in with parents periodically*—We often greet each other with a "How are you doing?" and hope that everything is fine. Yet, stopping for a moment and seeking out an honest answer can be revealing and helpful to parents. In congregations, parents often don't share their difficulties because these situations seem small compared to congregational members who are in the hospital, dealing with long-term illnesses, or may be even dying. Yet how will you know how parents are really doing if you don't ask them? Seek them out and find out what's happening in their lives as parents.

- *Show parents how your congregation helps them*— People who promote asset building often talk about the key niche that congregations have that no other place has. Congregations are one of the few institutions where children and teenagers have access to an intergenerational group of people. In school, sport teams, the arts, and clubs, they're

A CONGREGATION SUCCESS STORY

Emphasizing the Strengths of Blended Families

Some congregations take a strength-based approach to family ministry, which is what St. Giles Presbyterian Church in Richmond, Virginia, does. The congregation talks about how "stepfamilies are complex, but there is hope" and how the congregation can provide hope for these families.

The congregation offers stepparent couples to mentor other stepparents who may be new at this type of parenting. These mentor couples help blended families work through their challenges and find strategies on how to become a successful blended family.

The congregation also offers a blended family support group and a church family resource center that has resources (books and tapes) that family members can borrow.

almost always grouped by age. Unfortunately, few congregations take advantage of this unique advantage that they have. Those that do design occasional intergenerational events, intergenerational educational classes, or pair each child in the congregation with an adult in their church as a "faith partner" or "prayer partner." (See "The Power of Informal Relationships" in chapter 7 for ideas on how to start one of these partnership programs.)

Congregations are also places that are more likely to articulate and teach values. Many of the scripture texts have moral lessons, and classes often teach values, such as caring for others, being honest, and treating others fairly. Research shows that young people who participate in a congregation are more likely to care for others and are less likely to try risky and dangerous behaviors.[2]

The third unique strength of congregations is that they provide a wide range of structured activities for children, such as weekly religious education, service projects, youth groups, worship services, and mission trips. Children can develop meaningful relationships with the adults who are involved with these activities along with getting to know other children. They can also learn essential skills that will help them develop into competent adults, such as valuing diversity (asset #34), learning how to stand up for what they believe in (asset #28), and learning how to resist dangerous situations (asset #35).

Take stock of what your congregation offers to parents and their families. Try creating a list of what you offer each of these groups: children, teens, parents, and families. Often a congregation excels in providing opportunities for one or two of these groups but not for all four. Sometimes just adding one thing for a neglected group can make a big difference for some families.

• *Affirm parents when you witness their successful acts*— When you see evidence that parents are working hard with their children, affirm and encourage them. For example, if you see a parent talking with a child about not running in your congregation's hallways, affirm the parent. Sometimes it's also helpful to make light of the situation, such as saying: "You're teaching your child so well. Don't you wish kids listened to adults all the time?"

• *Help parents connect more with their kids*—Some congregations create opportunities for parents and children to play together. At St. Andrew's Presbyterian Church in Newport Beach, California, parents and their young children can attend a play group one day each week. There are play groups for children ages 12 to 24 months and another for children ages 22 to 33 months. Other congregations develop activities where parents and their teenagers talk about pertinent issues during a confirmation class or a youth activity.

• *Recognize parents in your bulletin and newsletter*— Make a list of all the parents of children and teenagers in your congregation. Be intentional about writing a paragraph about each one. (Highlight one parent per publication and continue this coverage until everyone has been recognized.) Mention not only what parents do as a vocation but also one or two of their favorite stories about being a parent. Many

A CONGREGATION SUCCESS STORY

Giving Clear Guidance and Support

When parents ask someone to be a godparent or the sponsor of their child, people don't always know what that entails. Is it just someone who shows up for the baptism ceremony? Or is the person supposed to do more?

Congregational leaders at Tarrytown United Methodist Church in Austin, Texas, developed clear guidelines on what a godparent or sponsor is and what the responsibilities are. Overall, the congregation says that godparents and sponsors are mentors and that they are making a commitment to be involved in the spiritual life of the child.

The congregation gives practical tips on how to be a godparent, such as staying in touch with the child, praying for the child and the parents of the child, focusing on their spiritual growth, and supporting the parents.

When parents, children, and godparents know what's expected of them, they're more likely to make informed decisions about becoming a godparent and then know what they need to do once they have made the commitment.

congregations now try to do this with children and youth so that other people in the congregation can get to know them. Do this with parents. If possible, include a photograph so that members of your congregation can connect names with faces.

• *Develop short, one-time volunteering opportunities*—Many parents are busy, yet many parents still want to participate. Create short, one-time volunteering opportunities in your congregation so that parents can contribute without having another responsibility added to their long list. Help parents succeed by creating small ways that they can contribute.

• *Ask parents about overscheduling*—One of the most difficult parts about being a successful parent is juggling the many demands on their family time. Talk with parents about

RESEARCH INSIGHTS

Parents Who Say They Do These Important Parenting Actions

We asked parents about 11 specific parenting actions that help children grow up healthy. (Each of these 11 parenting actions relates to specific assets within the developmental asset framework.) Here are the results:

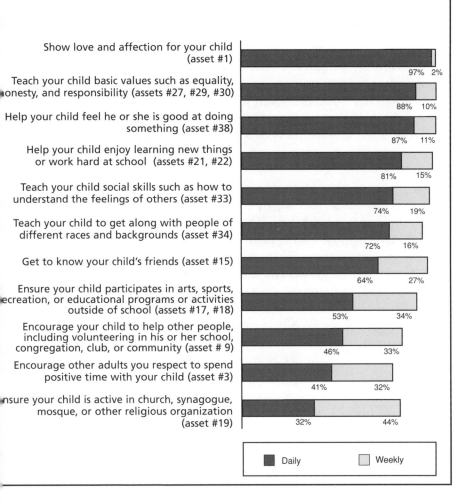

Show love and affection for your child (asset #1) — 97% 2%

Teach your child basic values such as equality, honesty, and responsibility (assets #27, #29, #30) — 88% 10%

Help your child feel he or she is good at doing something (asset #38) — 87% 11%

Help your child enjoy learning new things or work hard at school (assets #21, #22) — 81% 15%

Teach your child social skills such as how to understand the feelings of others (asset #33) — 74% 19%

Teach your child to get along with people of different races and backgrounds (asset #34) — 72% 16%

Get to know your child's friends (asset #15) — 64% 27%

Ensure your child participates in arts, sports, recreation, or educational programs or activities outside of school (assets #17, #18) — 53% 34%

Encourage your child to help other people, including volunteering in his or her school, congregation, club, or community (asset # 9) — 46% 33%

Encourage other adults you respect to spend positive time with your child (asset #3) — 41% 32%

Ensure your child is active in church, synagogue, mosque, or other religious organization (asset #19) — 32% 44%

■ Daily   ☐ Weekly

how your congregation's activities affect their overall scheduling. Sport teams often make it hard for parents, requiring them to attend practices or games when other congregational activities are taking place (including worship services).

In one area of Boston, the leadership of one congregation learned that families were not coming to Sunday morning worship services because parents had to take their kids to athletic games that were scheduled at the same time. The congregational leaders talked with leaders of other nearby congregations and discovered they were having the same difficulty. Together, the congregational leaders went to the athletic league to see if they could change the timing of these games. When they learned that there weren't enough fields for all the games, the congregational leaders and the athletic directors brainstormed ideas of how to solve the situation. When the congregational leaders suggested they raise funds to build lights so that the fields could have games at night, the athletic directors said that would solve the problem. Many congregations then held fundraisers and raised the money needed.

Your congregation doesn't usually need to go to such drastic measures to help parents with scheduling conflicts. Sometimes all that needs to happen is to reschedule certain congregational events near others so that parents don't need to take two trips—or to have a parenting class at the same time children go to religious education classes.

• *Take advantage of Mother's Day and Father's Day*— While these annual events can be sentimentalized or awkward for those who do not have a positive relationship with a parent, they can also be opportunities for people to focus on affirming and celebrating *all* parents, not just their own parents. Think of creative ways to highlight the ways that parents in the congregation are successful now—even before their children are old enough to take their mom or dad out for lunch on these special days. Highlight the important role that parents play in society and how everyone in the congregation can support parents and their children.

• *Focus on the positive*—Examine your existing parenting and family programs to determine whether they focus more on family problems or family strengths. Parents are more likely to attend events and classes that affirm the good work they're doing so far and teach how they can be even more effective as parents.

How to Help Parents Spend Time with Their Kids

Parents who spend time with their kids help their children grow up well. Most of the parents in our survey say they spend at least one hour a day talking, playing, or just being with their child. Yet some parents are much more likely to spend time with their kids than others.

Mothers are much more likely to be with their kids than fathers. African American parents also are more likely to hang out with their kids than white parents. How does your congregation create ways for parents to spend meaningful time with their children?

Unfortunately, many congregations fall into the trap of dividing families as soon as they come through the door. Infants and toddlers head to the nursery. Children and teenagers may go to a religious education class or even to a worship service that's designed just for them. Parents go to a worship service or someplace else, like out for a cup of coffee at a nearby coffee shop.

A certain amount of sending people to different places is okay. But how is your congregation helping parents connect with their kids? Do families have visible, important roles in worship (such as being ushers together or doing a scripture reading together)? Do you ever offer a family religious education class where moms, dads, and kids study scripture together? Do you ever have events for the whole family where they can talk together and have fun together?

Parents who feel successful often feel good about the times their families spend together. Congregations can provide a vital ministry by creating family opportunities that help parents and kids connect and enjoy one another's company.

Chapter 4

Finding #4: Most Parents Face Ongoing Challenges

ALTHOUGH MOST PARENTS feel successful as parents, they still face obstacles and challenges. In the *Building Strong Families* study, job demands and bickering among their children are the top things that parents say make parenting harder. The specific situations in which parents find themselves also shape the challenges they have.

Challenges Parents Face

When we asked parents about how much harder various issues make it to be a parent, of the six potential obstacles named, job demands topped the list. Seventeen percent of all parents surveyed said that work demands made their parenting very much harder and 33 percent said that their job made parenting somewhat harder.

Bickering among children was the second biggest challenge to parents. Forty-eight percent of parents said conflict among their children made their parenting very much or somewhat harder. This finding was unique to our survey since many other surveys emphasize the external challenges that parents face, such as shielding their children from danger or negative influences. Our survey revealed that dynamics within a family can also make parenting challenging.

A CONGREGATION SUCCESS STORY

Helping Unemployed Parents Find Jobs

Because most jobs go to people who are known to someone inside a company, Bethany Presbyterian Church in Seattle, Washington, created the Bethany JobLine where members can support each other in finding work.

The JobLine, which posts the names of parents and other people seeking work on a Web site, encourages people who know of a job posting to check the list to see if there are any potential matches. (Those seeking work are listed by name and job title desired.) Those seeking a job e-mail their resume, a short profile, and types of jobs being sought. Because of the high interest generated by JobLine, postings are only allowed for congregational members and those who regularly attend.

Two other significant stresses (which 41 percent of parents said made their parenting challenging) were over-scheduling (which included getting children's homework done) and the family's financial situation. The family's financial situation was much more stressful for parents who have a hard time buying the things that their family needs. Yet even among families who say they have no problem buying things their family needs and can also buy special things, 25 percent say that finances are an obstacle for them.

Thirty-four percent of parents say they feel pressured to buy things and that that pressure creates stress for them. Twenty-four percent said that being a single parent and having little support was a major challenge.

Different Challenges for Different Parents

Since some of the challenges are not as relevant to all parents, it's often helpful to compare the challenges that different subgroups of parents face.

Married parents say that job demands top their list of challenges. The percentage of married parents who say they have these challenges:

- job demands—50%
- sibling rivalry—49%
- overscheduling and children's homework—42%
- the family's financial situation—38%
- pressure to buy things—34%
- having little support—18%

Unmarried parents say that a lack of money tops their list of challenges. The percentage of unmarried parents who face these challenges:

- the family's financial situation—61%
- being a single parent and having little support—55%
- job demands—52%
- sibling rivalry—45%
- overscheduling and children's homework—37%
- pressure to buy things—36%

Parents who are financially stressed rank their list of challenges in a different order. This list pertains to parents who say that they have a hard time buying the things that their family needs. The percentage of financially stressed parents who face these challenges:

- the family's financial situation—77%
- job demands—59%
- sibling rivalry—54%
- being a single parent and having little support—52%
- overscheduling and children's homework—47%
- pressure to buy things—40%

Parents Who Have More Challenges

In addition to looking at the differences of challenges across different groups of parents, it's also helpful to see whether some parents experience more challenges than others. We combined all six challenges and analyzed which groups of parents are more likely to report that they found these issues make parenting harder.

We discovered that parents were more likely to experience challenges if they:

- have a household income of less than $50,000 a year or report having a hard time financially;
- have child-care arrangements other than staying at home with their child;
- have only a good, fair, or poor relationship with their spouse or parenting partner; or
- are unmarried.

These parents may have deeper challenges as parents, such as inadequate supports and allies in parenting, economic hardship that consumes parents' energy, and other responsibilities that make parenting harder, such as working outside the home or working multiple jobs.

The Daily Challenges of Parenting

It's one thing to say you experience certain challenges as a parent, and it's another thing to determine how well parents feel they're meeting these challenges. Although we did not specifically ask parents about how well they meet each of the six challenges, we asked a broad question about how well parents felt they "deal with the daily issues and challenges that come with being a parent."

Only about one out of four parents (23%) say they do extremely well in dealing with the daily challenges of parenting. Most (58%) say they do pretty well. One in five (19%) say they do poorly or just okay.

Certain groups of parents are more likely to say they deal well with the challenges of parenting than others. Those who are doing well:

- say they have no problem buying the things their family needs and they can also buy special things (compared to parents who say their family struggles financially).
- are Protestants (more than people with no religious preference).
- have an excellent relationship with their spouse or parenting partner.
- are African American parents (compared to white parents).

African American parents are twice as likely as white parents to say they handle the daily challenges of parenting extremely well (43% versus 20%). Parents who report having an excellent relationship with a spouse or partner are almost twice as likely to say they handle the daily challenges of parenting extremely well (28% versus 15%).

Why Parents Feel Dissatisfied

Besides asking about specific challenges they face in parenting, we also asked parents to indicate how much three different factors contributed to their not feeling satisfied with their parenting. The three factors we asked about included feeling overwhelmed, not having enough support, and feeling unprepared for certain parenting situations. Of these three options, feeling unprepared is the most common reason that parents feel dissatisfied. Close behind is feeling overwhelmed by everything.

Although most parents do not actively seek support from others for parenting, most do not perceive a lack of support

A CONGREGATION SUCCESS STORY

Creating a Strong Community for Parents

Epworth United Methodist Church in Berkeley, California, knows how important it is to create a sense of community for parents. Most of the congregation's teenage girls babysit for children in the congregation, which provides an important service for parents and babysitters while also helping teenagers get to know other parents and families in the congregation.

A group of senior members in the congregation have taken an intentional interest in young families so that families and seniors feel more connected. One older woman has taken one girl (who is now 16) Christmas shopping for the past seven years. Another older couple took kids to football games and got to know them (while giving the parents a break). The congregation also holds baby showers for each new baby, and everyone is encouraged to participate.

from family and friends as a major source of dissatisfaction with their parenting. This contradiction may reflect the reality that parents are not expecting a lot of support from others, so they don't see the lack of support as a significant problem. Or they may not seek support because they believe they will be judged instead of supported.

Several different groups of parents were more likely than others to feel dissatisfied because they are overwhelmed. Those who are more likely to feel overwhelmed included:

- those with only some college education (compared to college graduates).
- those having a hard time buying the things their family needs compared to those who say they have no problem buying the things their family needs and can even buy special things.
- mothers more than fathers.
- those with a fair or poor relationship with their

spouse or partner (compared to those with an excellent relationship).

- parents of 11- to 15-year-olds more than those of 5- to 10-year-olds.
- unmarried parents more than married parents.

How Your Congregation Can Ease Parenting Challenges

Depending on where they live and their circumstances, parents may have different challenges. The key to ministering to them effectively is knowing what their challenges are and being part of the solution. Consider these ideas.

- *Determine the challenges of parents in your congregation—* Create a short, written survey, asking parents what their challenges are. Or have a meeting with parents and form small groups to have these groups talk about the challenges. No matter how you find the information, learn about the unique challenges of the

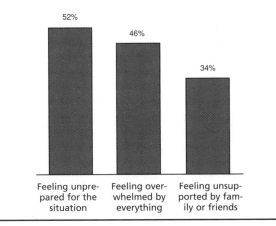

RESEARCH INSIGHTS

Why Parents Feel Dissatisfied

We asked parents what contributes to their dissatisfaction as parents. The percentage of parents who say that each factor contributes "very much" or "somewhat" to a time when they were not satisfied with what they did as a parent.

52%
46%
34%

Feeling unprepared for the situation
Feeling overwhelmed by everything
Feeling unsupported by family or friends

parents within your congregation. They may differ from other parents. (Or you may also discover some similarities.) Some congregations even get parents' feedback on an annual basis to ensure that the congregation is continuing to meet their needs.

• *Examine the challenges within challenges*—With job demands topping the list of challenges for most parents, consider what their needs may be in terms of child care. At St. John Lutheran Church in Vancouver, Washington, one woman quickly discovered that only some of the parents were having their needs met by the congregation's child-care program, which served children through first grade. By linking with a nearby school and parents who lived in an apartment building nearby, the congregation expanded the program to include all elementary school ages.

• *Encourage members to do their part*—As part of their faith commitment, ask members (both parents and nonparents) to provide encouragement to other parents they know who may be struggling. Building networks of care within your congregation can help parents feel supported.

• *Find out about the services your community provides*—Discover the places and people in your community who offer parents support. When you find parents who need specific supports that your community has, go with the parents to that place to link them to it and get them started. Many parents who are struggling often will not go alone to a place that they have been referred to. Having someone who can go with them the first time often makes a big difference.

• *Be open and flexible when parents become upset*—A parent called his minister in Michigan when his tenth grade son was caught with marijuana at school. Because the school had a zero-tolerance policy and suspended the boy for a semester, the dad didn't know what to do. He and his wife both worked and could not quit their jobs to supervise their son. The parents worried that if the boy stayed at home unsupervised, he would just sleep and do whatever he pleased. The minister became part of the solution. He offered to pick up the boy every day on his way to work and bring the boy to church with him. He had the boy do custodial work, and they also spent a lot of time talking about the boy's goals in life. The minister linked the boy with other adults who spent parts of their day at church. One elderly man taught the boy how to strip furniture. At the end of the semester, the boy was drug free and ready to go back to school with a healthy outlook for his future.

• *Use the developmental asset framework as a tool to help overwhelmed parents*—In Melvern, Arkansas, the First

RESEARCH INSIGHTS

Parents Who Feel Overwhelmed

Some parents feel much more overwhelmed than other parents. The percentage of parents who say "feeling overwhelmed by everything" is very much or somewhat a source of dissatisfaction for them:

GENDER
Mothers 51%
Fathers 44%

MARITAL STATUS
Married 44%
Unmarried 54%

ECONOMIC STRESS*
Much stress 60%
Some stress 48%
Little stress 42%

* Based on parents' selection of one: (a) I have a hard time buying the things my family needs, which we labeled as much stress; (b) I have just enough money for the things my family needs, which we labeled as some stress; or (c) I have no problem buying the things my family needs, and we can also buy special things, which we labeled as little stress.

United Methodist Church makes a special effort to share the developmental asset framework with parents who are feeling overwhelmed by issues that young people are facing. The congregational leadership says that the developmental asset framework "has been a wonderful tool to give parents a handle." Particularly when bad, scary news surrounds parents (such as a teenager committing suicide in the community), parents have found the developmental asset framework practical, concrete, and full of hope. See chapter 6 for specific ideas.

A CONGREGATION SUCCESS STORY

Helping Parents Adjust to Their New Role as Parents

A number of congregations have created ministries for new parents. At Faith Lutheran Church in Hastings, Nebraska, the congregation has a class called "Moms, Dads, and Babies." New parents and their babies get together weekly to talk about the joys and frustrations they are facing after the arrival of their baby. Not only do parents connect with each other but the facilitator teaches new parents how young children learn and how to interact more meaningfully with an infant.

The First Presbyterian Church of Orlando, Florida, recently set aside a special room for nursing mothers and parents of newborns. Called the "Seedling Nursery," this room is equipped with a television that broadcasts the worship service as parents rock their children, change their diapers, or nurse them during worship services. The congregation also offers an infant room for older infants who are ready to be separated from their parents during services. Other congregations with smaller budgets have wired speakers in the nursery so that parents can hear the worship service as they care for their child.

• *Seek out uninvolved parents on their turf*—Most likely you have some children and teenagers who get dropped off at your congregation for activities and you never (or rarely) see the parents. Call these parents and set up a time to visit them in their homes. Use this meeting as a way to gather information about how to support parents and make it easy for them to be involved. Take seriously the concerns parents raise about overscheduling. Work together to help parents find balance in family life.

• *Provide opportunities for parents to serve others*—When parents are struggling, our first reaction is to presume that they just need to be cared for themselves. So we may stop asking them to participate in ministries that help others. Yet, as Catholic writer Lief Kehrwald suggests, serving others can have a healing, renewing effect on parents and families. "Faced with so many problems of their own," Kehrwald writes, "many families are not motivated to serve others. Yet often, acts of selfless mercy can transform woes into healing as well as bring help to those in greater need."[1]

• *Partner with others in the community to help parents with their challenges*—Your congregation doesn't have to—and actually shouldn't try to—meet the needs of all parents. Connect with other resources in your community to provide the help that parents need. These may include family support services, a parent education network (such as Early Childhood and Family Education), a YMCA, or other resources. In Portsmouth, New Hampshire, parents and teenagers wanted a skateboard park built so that teenagers would have a place to hang out. St. Nicholas Greek Orthodox Church donated the one-acre lot behind its parish, and the city worked on procuring a $10,000 grant to get the park up and running. Teenagers chose the half-pipes and other amenities for the park, and many community residents volunteered their time to build the park.

Gaps That Add to the Parenting Challenge

Certain groups of parents clearly face more challenges, including those with weaker relationships with their spouse or parenting partner, those who are unmarried, and those with fewer financial resources. Each of these factors points to gaps in social and economic resources that add to the parenting challenge.

Strengthening these resources can make a positive difference in helping parents face the challenges that come their way. In the process, tap the strengths and resources that these parents already have (see, for example, Finding #3: Many Parents Feel Successful as Parents Most of the Time, in chapter 3) and the resources that they would value (see Finding #5: Many Things That Would Help Parents Are Easy Things Others Can Do, in chapter 5). These are helpful starting points for addressing the challenges that today's parents face.

Chapter 5

Finding #5: Many Things That Would Help Parents Are Easy Things Others Can Do

*P*ARENTS VALUE MANY simple ways that others can support them. Sometimes parents look for a bit of advice from a congregational leader—or another parent. Other times, they just long to hear someone say that they're doing a good job as parents. We asked parents about what specifically would help them in their parenting. The results suggest that parents may be more interested in building their informal, relational network of support, advice, and encouragement than in using formal programs, services, and resources.

What Parents Say Would Help Them

Our results show that there are a number of things that parents say would really help them as parents. The things they think would help them the most are not expensive or time consuming. Most emphasize informal supports that can be provided by congregational leaders and members, family, and friends. These include:

- getting parenting advice from their religious leaders, their child's teachers, and their doctors;
- people they trust spending a greater amount of positive time with their kids;
- talking with other parents about parenting issues;
- people telling them they're doing a good job as a parent; and
- having a more flexible work schedule.

At least one in four parents say that each of these opportunities would help them very much. In contrast, only about one in ten say that going to parenting classes or having more after-school programs and child-care options would help them very much.

Advice from Parents and Trusted Professionals

When it comes to getting parenting help or advice, parents say that they value input from both trusted professionals in their community and also from their friends or peers. Three-fourths of those surveyed say that advice from their child's religious leader, teacher, or doctor would help them very much or somewhat.

What kind of advice do parents want? When asked in an open-ended question, the three most common responses parents gave were:

- how to understand and deal with teenagers;
- how to have patience and understanding with their children; and
- opportunities to learn from parents who have been in similar situations.

Seventy-seven percent say that talking with other parents about parenting issues would help somewhat or very much. This desire is striking in that, only 20 percent of parents said it was very true that they turn to friends for advice and support in parenting. (See Finding #1 in chapter 1.) This suggests that parents may value this informal support, but too many parents do not feel comfortable or have opportunities for talking with other parents.

Other Adults Involved with Their Kids

A lot of research shows the importance of having many caring and responsible adults from outside the family involved in the lives of young people.[1] Our poll of parents also found that parents value the involvement of adults they trust in the lives of their children. Almost three of ten of our parents (71 percent) believe that such involvement would help them as parents. Indeed, when asked which one of eight resources would help them the most, "having people I trust . . . spend a greater amount of positive time with my kids" was their top choice.

A CONGREGATION SUCCESS STORY

Helping Parents Learn from Each Other

Parents learn from each other at Emmanuel Episcopal Church in Norwich, New York. The congregation offers a program called Progress in Parenting (PEP), which is made up of several groups. These include:

- parents of infants
- parents of toddlers
- parents of elementary-age children
- parents of teenagers
- parents of thresholders (young adults who have graduated from high school).

These groups meet to share, learn, and support one another through the process of parenting children of a specific age.

This priority is particularly high among white parents, with 25 percent selecting this as their top choice compared to only 14 percent of African American parents. This difference may reflect that parents of color face other pressing needs, but it also may show the lack of historic sense of "village" and shared responsibility within the U.S. Anglo and Euro-American culture.

In another Search Institute study, a majority of both young people and adults said it was important for adults outside the family to encourage school success, teach shared values, and teach respect for cultural differences. However, this study found a large gap between what people said was important and what they actually did. For example, although 73 percent of adults said it was most important for adults to teach shared values, only 58 percent said that they and adults they know actually do this.[2]

One of the major reasons other adults do not get involved with children and youth is that parents are not communicating their interest. About half of the adults surveyed said that they rarely or never asked parents for guidance for how to get involved with their children, and 29 percent of parents said that they rarely or never advise neighbors or other adults on how to engage with their children. The researchers concluded that: "Clearly most adults experience relatively weak social expectations and little or no encouragement to be involved with other people's kids in ways that promote the positive development of children and youth. But when adults do ask parents for engagement guidance, those adults report being more connected with kids."[3]

The Wish for Affirmation

Being affirmed rises to the top of things that parents say would really help them as parents. This desire is true across almost all groups of parents, regardless of marital status, income, or race. An important difference is that parents who

RESEARCH INSIGHTS

Religious Parents Are More Open to Assistance

When we compared parents who go to church with parents who rarely or never go to church, we discovered some major differences. Overall, religious parents are much more open to getting help from others and to connecting with others.

	Parents' Church Involvement	Helpful	Not Helpful
Getting help or advice from my child's religious leader, doctor, or teacher	Active	79%	21%
	Not active	68%	32%
Talking with other parents about parenting issues	Active	79%	21%
	Not active	69%	31%
People I trust . . . spending more positive time with my child	Active	74%	26%
	Not active	59%	41%
Others telling me I'm doing a good job as a parent	Active	69%	31%
	Not active	58%	42%
Parenting information I could get in private (books, television, etc.)	Active	60%	40%
	Not active	52%	48%
A more flexible work schedule	Active	50%	50%
	Not active	50%	50%
Going to a parenting class or workshop	Active	42%	58%
	Not active	29%	71%
More after-school programs or child-care options	Active	27%	73%
	Not active	34%	66%

are involved in a congregation, who still value affirmation, are apt to value three other actions more. (See the box "Religious Parents Are More Open to Assistance" on page 77.) Mothers also are more likely to say that affirmation would really help them. Seventy-three percent of mothers say this compared to only 56 percent of fathers.

This overall highly perceived value of being affirmed as parents likely reflects at least three important dynamics:

- It can be difficult to have perspective on how you're doing as a parent in the midst of the daily ebb and flow of life. Sometimes the results of parents' efforts don't become evident until several years later.
- If parents feel alone in the parenting task, they are unlikely to have people who can reflect with them about how it's going and articulate what they're doing well.
- The overall negative perceptions of parents and lack of attention to parenting strengths that were highlighted in the introduction to Finding #3 (chapter 3) likely leave parents second-guessing themselves and believing that, despite their best efforts, they really are not doing well. In another Search Institute study of families who live in distressed communities, the researchers noted that "these families were so accustomed to being scrutinized in terms of what they were not doing, or what they were doing wrong, that they didn't even know how much they were doing well on behalf of their children."[4]

Work Flexibility of Parents

Balancing work and family appears to be an ongoing challenge for the parents we surveyed. The top challenge for parents (from Finding #4) was job demands. It is not surprising, then, that 50 percent of parents also say a more flexible work schedule would help them as parents.

Work flexibility is particularly valued by those in more difficult economic circumstances. Among parents who

A CONGREGATION SUCCESS STORY

Making Life Easier for Busy Parents

Parents at Old River Terrace United Methodist Church in Channelview, Texas, never have to worry about what to cook for dinner (or breakfast or lunch). The congregation publishes easy-to-make, affordable recipes for busy parents on its Web site. Parents can quickly find a recipe (along with a color photo to entice them to try it) and also submit their favorite recipes to be posted on the Web site.

As parents cook, they can download coloring pages, mazes, games, and crafts for their kids to do. (The congregation also has these on their family fun Web site.) Kids interested in cooking can try the recipes posted just for them.

say they struggle financially, 40 percent say that a more flexible work schedule would help them very much compared to only 22 percent of parents who say they don't have financial struggles.

A related item was after-school care and child care. Although this item received relatively low ratings, it may be because our sample underrepresents parents of young children. Of the parents we surveyed, 63 percent say they do not need child care. Only 16 percent said they used child care. Of parents who do use child care, 24 percent said that more after-school and child-care options would help them very much. This compares to only 10 percent of other parents.

Differences are significant with families who struggle financially. Twenty-four percent of parents who say their family is having a hard time financially say that more after-school and child-care options would help them very much, and another 18 percent said that it would help them somewhat. This compares to only 9 percent of parents who say they are doing well financially.

Information for Personal Use

The lower ratings for information for use in private (such as books, television, or the Internet) is a reminder that information by itself is not as powerful as information within the context of relationship. Yet, parents who go to a congregation are much more likely to see informational resources as a help, especially compared to parents who don't go to a congregation. While 60 percent of parents who are part of a congregation say this type of information would be helpful for their parenting, only 40 percent of parents who don't participate in a congregation agree.

Parents facing financial stress and those who are unmarried appear to particularly value this type of information. In your congregation, it may be helpful to view private information on parenting as supplementary, not as a substitute for information and supports that are shared through dialogue and relationships. Like any type of strategy, it's typically most effective to do a number of strategies simultaneously since some parents respond to certain strategies over others.

Parenting Classes and Workshops

Parenting classes and workshops are another strategy to support parents. Although most parents we polled place more emphasis on informal supports, 40 percent of parents very much or somewhat value the opportunity for parenting classes and workshops. These percentages are even higher for certain groups:

- African American parents are more likely to say that these opportunities would help them very much or somewhat. Forty-nine percent of African American parents say this compared to only 28 percent of white parents.

- Almost half of unmarried parents (47%) would value these opportunities. This compared to 38 percent of married parents.

It's important to consider whether intentionally integrating some of the informal things that parents value into classes and workshops would enhance their value to parents. For example, do parents perceive (perhaps based on experience) that learning opportunities are only for dealing with problems or to tell parents what they're not doing well? How would it make a difference to ensure that these classes affirm parents and give them opportunities to learn from each other?

How Your Congregation Can Make a Difference for Parents

Little things mean a lot to parents, and your congregation can offer parents support just by getting to know them and by being interested in their family lives. You also can go deeper and provide more for parents. Consider these ideas:

- *Ask the parents*—A first step in helping parents know that your congregation is paying attention is to ask them what they want, need, and

> **A CONGREGATION SUCCESS STORY**
>
> *Parenting Resources to Read and Discuss*
>
> Faith Baptist Church in Grayslake, Illinois, posts Christian parenting books on its Web site. Listed in the "parents' library" are six current books parents can choose from. Each book has its cover pictured and includes an explanatory paragraph about the book.

value. What do the parents in your congregation and community value? Where do they feel a need for support or information?[5] Instead of having an "if we build it, they will come"
attitude, adopt an attitude of "Let them build it, and we will
come to them."

• *Create an annual parent recognition event or award*—
Highlight parents who are model parents and who are succeeding as parents despite the odds. For example, recognize
parents who involve their families in family service projects,
for ensuring that their children finish their homework most
of the time, for connecting their children with extended family, and for transporting their kids to practices, games, and
lessons. Recognize parents by developing an annual dinner in
honor of parents or affirm them in smaller ways, such as recognizing them during a worship service or mentioning their
efforts in your congregational bulletin or congregational
newsletter.

• *Have your clergy say what they offer parents*—Some
ministers counsel parents and families. Some enjoy visiting
families in their homes. A few will lead occasional classes or
workshops. You don't need a brochure of what your congregational leadership offers, but it's helpful to tell parents from
time to time how your religious leadership can assist them.

• *Find ways to link congregational members with individual family members*—Determine how more people in your
congregation can get to know the kids and parents in your
congregation. At St. John Lutheran Church in Idaho Falls,
Idaho, the youth group was struggling and so was the
Fellowship Club (which was a group of people who are 55
and older). The congregation decided to have the two groups
meet at the same time. The two groups first met separately to
take care of their individual needs, and then they got together
for snacks, talking, and games. Small groups (of both young
people and older people) formed to play Pinochle, Dominoes,
and other board games. The Fellowship Club heard that two
of the youth in the youth group wanted to go to a leadership
conference but didn't have the money to do so. Because of

the strong relationships that had formed, members of the Fellowship Club created a fund-raiser and raised the money for them to go. This was a big boost for the parents who wanted their kids to have this opportunity but didn't have the financial resources to send them.

• *Get parents together to talk about work issues*—Have parents tell about their work situation and about how well they balance their work and family life. Be clear that this is not a gripe session but a sharing and learning session. Bringing parents together may help them find ways to support one another. For example, one mother learned that another parent who lived nearby worked a night shift every Friday night and could never find child care for her children. The mother suggested that the working parent drop off the children at her house on Friday evening before work and that she would put all the children to bed so they could maintain their bedtime routines. The parent then picked her children up Saturday morning after work.

• *Create parenting groups by linking families with similar backgrounds*—Some congregations create parent groups by the age of children or the number of children. Others create parent groups by family type, such as blended families, single-parent families, and dual-income families. At St. Luke's Methodist Church in Indianapolis, the congregation has a group called Jesse's Street, which is a group for parents who have children with special needs. At Bon Air Baptist Church in Richmond, Virginia, there's a support group for parents of autistic children. Because St. Luke Presbyterian Church in Minnetonka, Minnesota, had many parents who had adopted children internationally, the congregation periodically sponsored events where the families got together.

• *Provide stimulating, helpful materials on parenting*—Some congregations create a small library for parents. Others create book-study groups for parents. Some have free brochures that parents can take, such as Care Notes or other brochures on parenting and family life that they order from their denominational publisher. Congregations that have

RESEARCH INSIGHTS

What Would Really Help Parents

We asked parents how much each of these eight things would help them as parents. Here is what they said:

	Very Much	Somewhat	Not Helpful
Others telling me I'm doing a good job as a parent	31%	36%	33%
Getting help or advice from my child's religious leader, doctor, or teacher	29%	47%	24%
People I trust . . . spending more positive time with my child	29%	42%	29%
A more flexible work schedule	27%	23%	50%
Talking with other parents about parenting issues	24%	53%	23%
Parenting information I could get in private (books, television, etc.)	16%	42%	42%
More after-school programs or child-care options	13%	15%	72%
Going to a parenting class or workshop	12%	28%	60%

become serious about asset building and using the developmental asset framework have photocopied bulletin inserts that family members and other congregational leaders can use. (These bulletin inserts can be found on pages 171-91 of the book *Building Assets in Congregations*.)[6]

• *Offer parents opportunities to fellowship and serve together*—Sometimes parents just need opportunities to get to know each other a little better. It's not safe to assume that parents have built relationships with each other simply because their children are in the same Sunday school class or youth group. Connecting opportunities can include standard fellowship opportunities such as dinners, special events, and retreats. It's also important to remember that service and leadership opportunities can be particularly powerful shared experiences through which deep bonds can form.

• *Create a child-care directory of your community*—Parents who are seeking child care often don't know all their options. Create a task force of parents interested in this issue to develop a child-care directory of child-care centers and families that offer child care. (Often families that offer child care in their home don't have much opportunity to get the word out about their services.) Also consider creating a babysitting directory of the teenagers and interested adults in your congregation.

• *Develop parenting study groups*—Have parents come together regularly to discuss parenting issues. Focus on how parents can build strengths rather than emphasizing the problems that families and children face. Work on building community in these parenting groups so parents develop a supportive network.

• *Encourage religious education teachers to get to know their students and their students' parents*—Build community and connections to parents by having other adults in your congregation get to know their names and a little about them. Parents often are interested in how their children are doing in religious education, confirmation, and other congregational activities, so giving them some feedback while also taking the time to talk with them often is helpful and appreciated.

• *Affirm parents' efforts*—Encourage parents to continue making a difference in the lives of their children. From time to time, remind your congregational members to affirm what parents do.

• *Make your congregation more family friendly*—Often congregations have certain areas that are family friendly, such as the nursery or a religious education classroom for young children. Add age-appropriate books and toys for children to play with in some of the areas where your congregation gets together for fellowship and casual times. (Sometimes just adding a basket of toys near the chairs in a waiting area can be a welcome addition to parents.) Encourage parents to use the nursery even when it's not staffed (not to drop off their children, but to play with their children). Along the hallway walls of your church, consider hanging up family pictures that children have drawn.

Differences in Parents' Priorities

In examining what parents say would really help them, it's important to recognize that parents have different priorities depending on their life circumstances. Because of that, there is not a single strategy or resource that, if they had it, would meet the needs of all parents. Rather, these findings suggest that, within a congregation, a wide range of formal and informal supports and opportunities are needed that respond to the life situations and personal styles of diverse parents across the first two decades of their children's lives. Use the findings from this study as a springboard for dialogue with the parents in your congregation to find out what will best meet their needs and will strengthen their families.

Chapter 6

Equipping and Supporting Parents

THE FIVE FINDINGS from our study of parents across the United States invite you to reflect on the ways your congregations already does—and could—equip parents. Your congregation already has a strong start. It does a number of things well for parents, and you can do even more. This doesn't mean you need to start new programs, hire additional staff, or tap into resources that you don't have. It's about more effectively using what you do have and building on your strengths.

An Effective Tool for Helping Parents

Many congregations have started using the developmental asset framework as the major tool for building on their strengths to help parents and young people. Since developmental assets prevent risky behaviors, promote positive behaviors, and help kids bounce back from difficulties as outlined in the introduction, many congregations have found that building assets has given their congregation new life while also energizing parents.

At Trinity Lutheran Church in Bellevue, Washington, families come together weekly to meet for dinner at 5:45. After dinner, the congregation has an open-mike time where par-

A CONGREGATION SUCCESS STORY

Offer Meaningful Classes for Parents

Parents have countless opportunities to learn more at Christ Church of Oak Brook, Illinois. The congregation has a parenting program that includes parenting courses and one-session classes, parent forums, library resources, and parenting resources for sale. All classes are lead by the congregation's paid leadership.
Parenting classes include:

- Contact (a fellowship and teaching group for parents who want to build strong, faith-based families);
- A single parent discussion group;
- The meaning and significance of infant baptism; and
- Help! I'm the Parent of an Adolescent.

The congregation also has a MOPS (Mothers of Pre-Schoolers) group. A number of congregations offer MOPS, which is an international, nondenominational, Christian organization devoted to meeting the distinct needs of mothers parenting 3- to 5-year olds.

ents and their kids come forward to tell positive things about each other. One father, wearing a bright red shirt, came forward and said, "I know that my daughter's face is as red as my shirt right now, but I just wanted to tell you that she won a horse competition last week, and I am so proud of her." The daughter was embarrassed, but she went back to school the next day feeling cared for by her dad and knowing he was proud of her.

After open-mike time, a short program begins. The program, called Families Under Construction, focuses on one category of developmental assets each week (such as support or empowerment). After a brief presentation, families do an active learning activity to reinforce what they just learned.

Because of this format, parents are excited to come to this congregation. They're connecting with other parents, getting to know their kids' peers, and learning practical ways to raise good kids.

Congregational leaders at St. Raymond Catholic Church in Menlo Park, California, present the developmental asset framework to single parents in the parent support group, Good Parents Café. As leaders illustrate the many different ways to build assets and the many people who can do their part, parents relax, realizing that they can build assets in their children and that they have many partners to help them.

Seven congregations in Adams County, Illinois, have become intentional about building developmental assets in young people and their parents. Luther Memorial Church, Union United Methodist, First Union Congregational, Seventh-Day Adventist, Our Redeemer Lutheran, Salem Evangelical United Church of Christ, and First Presbyterian Church have all implemented more intergenerational activities to provide support for parents and their children. They're also helping parents link with appropriate services within the community.

"The developmental assets model gave focus to our congregational work," says Enid Norman, when she worked for ASAP, a Chicago community organization that created and supported collaborations among congregations. "We felt that the assets were an ideal fit with what we wanted to do."[1] Many congregations are finding that building assets is a key way to help parents raise successful kids.

The Strength of the Developmental Assets Framework

Why does an asset-building approach help parents be more effective? Because developmental assets work. For years, researchers have pointed to poverty and race as some of the major reasons parents haven't been effective. New research from Search Institute now shows that not all children who live in poverty and who are members of a minority groups are destined for failure. Some, despite the difficulties their families face, actually turn out well. What makes the most difference? Developmental assets.[2]

What about children who are from middle- or upper-class homes? Developmental assets, again, are the difference in what separates children who succeed from those who don't. The same is true for young people of all races and from all types of families, whether they live in single-parent families, two-parent families, or blended families.[3] Scientific research on almost two million young people across the United States has proved that developmental assets help kids succeed.

Parents who build developmental assets in their children are helping them grow up well. Parents who surround their children with other asset builders (such as helpful members of your congregation, caring teachers, and friendly neighbors) can help their kids even more. Parents who attend asset-building congregations that are located in asset-building school districts and asset-building communities have seen the long-term, positive effects of children succeeding as everyone rallies around the children and builds their developmental assets.

Congregations, communities, and school districts who have been building assets for a number of years have seen that it's not only essential for everyone to build assets in young people but also to support and equip parents. Across the country, congregations, communities, and school districts are developing creative ways to uplift and support parents in their critical role of parenting and by equipping them with the essential skills they need to really help their kids succeed. These places have seen that when parents succeed, children are more likely to succeed. That's good for parents. That's good for young people, and that's good for your congregation.

Ten Steps for Equipping Parents as Asset Builders

Congregations often are most successful in helping parents learn the developmental asset framework by giving parents bite-size bits of information about assets. Many who have succeeded in doing so have typically followed these ten steps.

Step 1: Learn as much as you can about developmental assets—You will be much more effective in supporting and equipping parents with the developmental asset framework if you know about the framework first. Although asset building is a key strategy for supporting and equipping parents, parents need to hear that they are not the only asset builders in their children's lives. The assets provide a framework for action that encourages *all* of your congregational leaders and members to make a difference for young people and their parents. It's a way of uniting everyone so that parents, their children, and your members all can thrive and connect with each other in more meaningful ways. Asset building is an approach, not a program.

Three introductory resources (which are fairly short and easy to use) include *The Asset Approach,* an eight-page introduction to the developmental asset framework; *Tapping the Potential,* a 16-page booklet on how congregations can build assets; and *What Kids Need to Succeed,* a 224-page book that presents the asset framework in an easy-to-understand way and includes more than 900 ideas, including how congregations can build each of the 40 developmental assets. The Search Institute Web site also presents a helpful overview of the asset framework at www.search-institute.org/assets.

As you become more familiar with developmental assets, consider using a congregational resource that shows how to integrate asset building into all aspects of congregational life. *Building Assets in Congregations* presents an overview of how to transform your entire congregation into an asset-building congregation. This practical book includes worksheets for assessing and planning your current priorities and programs, tips for creating intergenerational programs and parent workshops, and ten reproducible bulletin inserts. Some congregational leaders even attend Search Institute's annual Healthy Communities • Healthy Youth conference, which has a congregational track of workshops on asset

RESEARCH INSIGHTS

Perceptions of Parents and Other Adults of How Congregations Support Parents and Families

Search Institute researchers asked parents and other adults in 15 congregations how well their congregation is doing in supporting parents and families. Here are the percentages of parents with children under 18 and other adults who say their congregation does very or extremely well in each area.[4]

	Parents with Children	Other Adults
Supporting families in times of change and crisis	36%	45%
Involving parents in planning and leading programs and activities for children and youth	36%	40%
Providing opportunities for families to serve others together	30%	32%
Teaching parents to talk about faith with their children	28%	26%
Strengthening relationships between parents and their children	23%	30%
Helping parents build a strong relationship with their spouse or parenting partner	21%	26%
Supporting families in doing religious rituals or ceremonies at home	21%	20%

building. All of these resources are available through Search Institute of Minneapolis.

Step 2: Connect parenting and faith—Though the asset framework is not explicitly grounded in the Christian faith and language, most parents and congregational leaders quickly find important connections. In the process, they discover that the asset framework helps them reflect in new ways on faith, discipleship, and parenting.

For these connections to emerge, it is helpful first to articulate key themes in Christian parenting, since many parents may not have reflected in any depth on how their faith shapes their parenting practices and priorities. Then when you introduce the developmental assets, parents and others will be better equipped to identify and articulate the areas of compatibility between faith and asset building. This articulation also provides the context for why you are doing asset building with parents in your congregation.

Consider engaging parents and other adults in dialogue around the following kinds of questions (and keep track of their responses):

• What responsibilities has God given to Christian parents?

• What kinds of things do parents do because of their Christian faith?

• In what ways is Christian parenting similar to and different from parenting in general?

• How do basic parenting tasks such as showing children love, disciplining children, and ensuring that children develop mentally, spiritually, socially, physically, and emotionally relate to Christian parenting?

• Who else besides parents has a responsibility and calling to nurture children and teenagers?

These kinds of questions may be challenging for many parents, since they may not have had opportunities to reflect on these issues. Furthermore, unless your congregation has a tradition of addressing family and parenting issues from a faith perspective, they may be surprised that you're even raising the questions. Yet integrating parenting and faith not only brings new perspectives and strength to parents but also provides a rationale for addressing asset building with parents in the faith community. Some themes that may emerge in these conversations include the following:

• Parents are called to "impress [God's commandments] on your children. Talk about them when you sit at home and when you walk along the road, when you lie down and when you get up" (Deuteronomy 6:7 NIV).

• Parents play a central role in helping their children receive the gift of faith as they participate in the life of the faith community and as they share the stories, beliefs, and expectations of the Christian faith.

• Faith affects all aspects of parenting as parents seek to model Christian teachings and live as God would have them live.

A CONGREGATION SUCCESS STORY

Make Your Parent Offerings Cost Effective

New Life Counseling, a Christ-centered counseling ministry of Arizona Baptist Children's Services, provides economical counseling sessions for parents. Fees range from $35 to $75 a session, and are based on family income. For parents who can't afford the fee, counselors attempt to subsidize the counseling through congregational gifts.

Counselors are trained in many specialty areas (such as single parenting, anger issues, depression, stress, grief and loss, divorce, and relationship issues) with a biblical approach. Counselors meet with parents in a number of locations including Trinity Baptist Church in Casa Grande and at the Sierra Vista Nazarene Church in Sierra Vista.

• Parents are imperfect and need God's grace and forgiveness.

• Parents have a particular responsibility to nurture children, but all in the community of faith share a responsibility to care for, guide, and nurture one another, including children and teenagers.

Step 3: Begin by getting parents interested—Parents want their children and teenagers to grow up well, and there's a multitude of information about the "right way" to parent. Much of this information is from experts who are psychologists, medical doctors, professors in child development, and parents themselves. Unfortunately, a lot of this information can be contradictory when you set it side by side, and parents often aren't sure which advice is best.

Begin by asking parents the central question: How do you parent kids so that they succeed in life? Some parents will have a few ideas, but many parents will be intrigued by the question and want to know the answer. Without using any of the developmental asset language, talk about how researchers have identified key building blocks that all children and teenagers need to succeed and that they surveyed almost two million young people across the United States and found that these building blocks do help kids succeed. You can then give a couple of examples of these building blocks from the list of the 40 developmental assets, such as youth programs, a sense of purpose, honesty, and service to others. (See the appendix for the five lists of developmental assets for five age groups: infants, toddlers, preschoolers, elementary-age children, and middle and highschool young people. Use the list for middle and highschool young people for examples of asset names.)

Step 4: Show the power of these building blocks—Present the research evidence behind these building blocks. Talk about the protective power of the building blocks and how young people who have more of these building blocks are much less likely to participate in dangerous and risky behaviors, such as using alcohol, becoming violent, having sexual intercourse as a teenager, and stealing. Highlight that there are 24 risky behaviors that researchers have measured against these key building blocks, and young people are less likely to do any of these 24 risky behaviors as they acquire more of these building blocks.

RESEARCH INSIGHTS

Largest Gaps for Congregations Supporting Parents and Families

What young people and adults in eight pilot congregations say is important is different from what they experience. Here are the top five major gaps (between ranking it as a congregational priority and the reality) for young people and adults.[5]

Youth	Adults
1. Strengthening relationships between parents and their children	1. Teaching parents to talk about faith with their children
2. Helping parents build a strong relationship with their spouse or parenting partner. (tie)	2. Strengthening relationships between parents and their children
2. Teaching parents to talk about faith with their children. (tie)	3. Helping parents build a strong relationship with their spouse or parenting partner
3. Providing parents with support and information to help them be better parents	4. Caring for and supporting families in times of change and/or crisis
4. Caring for and supporting families in times of change and/or crisis. (tie)	5. Providing parents with support and information to help them be better parents
4. Connecting parents with other adults who can support and guide them as parents. (tie)	
5. Offering fun and/or meaningful activities for families to do together	

Emphasize how these building blocks also encourage young people to act in positive ways that we value. When young people have more of these building blocks, they are more likely to succeed in school, help others, and take leadership roles. Researchers have measured eight specific behaviors that increase as the number of these building blocks goes up in young people.

Talk about how important it is for young people to cope and be able to bounce back from difficulties. What helps young people rebound after a traumatic event or a difficult situation? These building blocks. The more of these building blocks that young people have, the more likely they are to get up from being knocked down and try again.

Step 5: Talk about what kids need around them and inside them—The developmental asset framework includes two broad categories: external assets and internal assets. Instead of calling these things "assets," continue to use the phrase "building blocks." External building blocks are the people, programs, organizations, and congregations that surround young people. The more young people and their parents have effective people, programs, and places around them, the more likely they are to grow up to be caring and successful. The first 20 assets make up the category of external assets. Present this idea by talking about what kids and families need around them to succeed.

Internal building blocks (or assets) are the commitments, values, and passions that young people need to tap within themselves to grow up well. Young people can't just access these things inside themselves, they need adults to help them develop and master these important traits. The last 20 assets are the internal assets. Many congregations talk about these internal assets as positive values, skills, and character traits that children and their parents need to develop well.

Step 6: Introduce the language of developmental assets— After parents know about the power of these building blocks and the two broad categories (external and internal), begin to introduce them to the language of asset building. Approach the language from where parents are. Most parents think about assets as money or wealth. Use the phrase "developmental assets" as a way of pointing out the rich opportunities that parents and their kids have around them and inside them. The building blocks of healthy development help create asset-rich kids and asset-rich parents.

Step 7: Explain the developmental asset framework—Distribute to parents the list of the 40 developmental assets. Make sure that parents get the list that fits the age of their children. That means some parents will get more than one list if they have multiple children of different ages. Photocopy the lists of assets from the appendix in this book or download the lists from www.search-institute.org/assets as pdf or html files. These lists are available in both English and Spanish.

When you explain the developmental asset framework, address the idea that this may seem overwhelming at first. While it is true that there are 40 building blocks, which are the 40 developmental assets, parents aren't expected to go home and begin building all 40 right away. Also parents aren't the only ones who should build assets. People within your congregation, teachers at school, neighbors, coaches, and community residents should also help. Explain that this list is meant to help parents start thinking about themselves as asset builders.

Reiterate the two broad categories: external and internal assets. Then begin addressing the eight categories of assets. Support, empowerment, boundaries and expectations, and constructive use of time are the four categories that make up the external assets. Commitment to learning, positive values, social competencies, and positive identity are the four categories that make up the internal assets.

Step 8: Link asset building with your congregation's language, beliefs, priorities, and practices—Step #2 sought to help parents begin to see parenting as integrally connected to their Christian faith. Once they begin understanding the developmental assets, it's time to return to those earlier conversations to extend the connections between Christian parenting and asset building. Remind people of the earlier conversations, and ask them to identify connections between the tasks and goals of Christian parenting and the asset-building approach. People approach this task in a number of different ways. Here are some options:

• Look for similarities between major themes of Christian parenting and asset building. For example, you may note that when infants are dedicated or baptized, parents, sponsors, and other congregation members commit to nurturing their faith and growth. The assets provide a tool to make these broad commitments more concrete and actionable.

• Find links through stories. Ask people to talk about an experience or a person that has profoundly affected them and their faith. Then have them analyze the same story through an asset-building lens. Or analyze stories in Scripture to see which developmental assets were present.

• Link scripture passages with the developmental assets. Many assets and asset-building themes are clearly related to scripture passages. Help parents see the connections. As a springboard, use the list of passages for each asset that is found in the appendix on pages 136-37.

As you help parents make these connections, avoid getting lost in all the details and losing the big picture. It may be better to emphasize the links between faith and the eight categories of assets than to try to link to all 40 individual assets. For example, how are parents called by faith to show support and care to children or to shape their identity?

Similarly, it is important not to become legalistic with the asset framework. There are, for example, many ways that people of faith are encouraged to set boundaries that are entirely consistent with but not explicitly addressed by the framework. Use the framework as a guide and stimulus for reflection and discussion. Not only will this approach open up additional possibilities but it also will allow you to keep using the framework, even if some elements do not fully resonate with someone's theology or perspective.

Finally, don't presume or give the impression that asset building replaces faith nurture. Yes, they overlap and are complementary. But asset building does not supersede your efforts to nurture faith in children, youth, parents, and families. Rather, it can enrich and deepen you faith-building efforts.

Step 9: Tell parents how your congregation will provide more information about asset building—Talk about how your congregation will begin to educate parents about these developmental assets over the next few months or years. Some congregations focus on one category of developmental assets each month during the school year (with the first month focusing on the general idea of asset building). Then some congregations begin to go more in-depth with asset building the next year by focusing on a specific asset one week at a time. They coordinate their efforts so that parents, children, and members are learning about asset building through worship, Christian education, and congregational materials (such as your congregational newsletter and/or bulletin).

Step 10: Keep asset building in the forefront of all your congregational planning—As you create your plans for worship, Christian education, family ministry, community outreach, mission, service, music, and the other ministry areas of your congregation, talk about what each area can do to support and equip parents and congregational members to be asset builders. Chapter 7 presents many ideas about how to do this. What's essential is to keep asset building as an agenda item so that it doesn't fall through the cracks or get relegated to only one congregational leader or one ministry area.

Your Congregation's Emphases on Parents and Families

As your congregation begins to support and equip parents, two questions most likely will arise. How well is your congregation currently ministering to parents and their children? What priorities does your congregation have for parents and their children? Because these simple questions have answers that aren't easy to discover in a systematic and scientific way, Search Institute has designed an affordable survey that offers a wealth of information about your congregation. Titled *Building Assets, Strengthening Faith,* this survey not only asks adults about their own perceptions of your congregation and its priorities but also asks young people, which many congregational surveys overlook.

> ## A CONGREGATION SUCCESS STORY
>
> ### *Connect with Established Resources*
>
> Many denominational offices have high-quality services and materials that parents often don't know about. Floris United Methodist Church in Herndon, Virginia, not only works with families of high schoolers who are looking for colleges and scholarships, they also link these families to their denominational resources. For example, the congregation connects families with the United Methodist General Board of Higher Education to receive the free 28-page resource for choosing a college. (The congregation has a Web site link to the General Board to make it easy for families to request the booklet.) The congregation also highlights a couple of scholarship opportunities, such as the United Methodist Scholarship Program (through the United Methodist General Board of Higher Education) and the Richard S. Smith and David W. Self Scholarships (through the United Methodist National Youth Ministry Organization).

The types of questions that are asked in this survey include:

• *Context*—Your congregation's basic characteristics are unique because of your congregation's identity, character, and people. This portion of the survey examines individuals (including their age, gender, ethnicity, education, and level of involvement), and families (composition and level of faith commitment). Thus, the survey gives a broad picture of the individuals and families in your congregation—information that many congregations do not have readily available.

• *Your congregational approach*—This survey examines two types of approaches your congregation uses in its work with parents, children, youth, and families. The first is faith and spiritual development. This survey includes a number of items that build on Search Institute's previous research on congregational factors that contribute to growth in faith among young people and adults. The second is asset building. What are the asset-building qualities of your congregation? Although this survey does not measure the number of developmental assets that young people in your congregation have, it examines your congregation's approach to asset building.

These two approaches—spiritual development and asset building—are mutually reinforcing lenses through which you can examine your congregation's priorities and strengths. Some of the same activities that nurture faith also build assets and vice versa. Emerging research confirms that young people with higher asset levels are also more likely to emphasize spiritual development.

• *Settings*—This survey examines four broad settings in which spiritual development and asset building are encouraged by congregations. Whereas many congregations have historically focused most of their attention on the specific programs for parents, children, and youth, this model proposes that all areas of congregational life and mission have the potential for asset building and spiritual development. The four broad settings include: family engagement, child and youth engagement, congregationwide engagement, and community engagement.

• *Dynamics*—Several congregational dynamics become crosscutting threads in each setting. It's important, therefore, to weave spiritual development and asset-building strategies into each of these dynamics, all of which are addressed in the survey. This includes: leadership and processes, environment, relationships, rituals, and programs and practices. Each of these five dynamics interacts with the others. For example, your congregation could purchase the best curriculum available for Christian education, but it might be ineffective if there are not quality relationships between leaders and participants or if the environment for learning is chaotic or lacks a sense of mutual trust.

• *Potential areas of impact*—Finally, the survey provides respondents' perceptions of how your congregation is affecting them, their family, and your community. It also asks for their perceptions of congregational vitality.

Once your congregation has tabulated the data, you will receive a detailed report as well as suggestions for how to use the report in planning. This report will not only highlight all your results but also be a useful tool for transforming your congregation to be more effective for parents, children, youth, and families. A number of congregations have already used this helpful tool, and a few of the results from the first pilot are included in the "Research Insights" boxes of this chapter. These congregations are now using their data to help them plan their next steps and make more effective changes.

To receive more information about this congregational survey (including costs and timelines), visit www.search-institute.org/congregations. In early testing with congregations and individuals, Search Institute found that the vast majority of both youth and adults found the survey to be interesting, relevant, and helpful to their congregation. People want to tell about their experiences and priorities for their congregation. Most see it as an opportunity, not just something else they're being asked to do.

Congregational Realities for Parents

What parents want and what they actually get in a congregation can be two very different things. In a study of 1,592 people from 15 field test congregations, Search

Institute researchers found widespread concerns in areas such as the following:

1. teaching parents to talk about faith with their children;
2. strengthening relationships between parents and their children;
3. helping parents build a strong relationship with their spouse or parenting partner;
4. teaching children and youth spiritual practices, such as prayer or meditation.[6]

Unfortunately, many congregations come up short in supporting and equipping parents at all. In a survey of 500 religious youth workers, only 6 percent say they support and educated parents very well. (The good news, however, was that 45 percent say that supporting and educating parents is an important goal, and 59 percent are interested in training and resources in this area.)[7] In a study of 11,000 adults and young people in six major Christian denominations, only 9 percent of congregations provide education for parents of youth on effective parenting or communication.[8]

Your Congregation's Strengths

Although some of the realities for parents may not be positive, your congregations can support parents and equip them with the essential skills to parent their children well. Your congregation already is doing a number of things well, and a helpful strategy is to build on what's working while you also fill in the gaps.

Many congregations attempt to determine their strengths by the programs they offer. Yet programming isn't what makes you effective and strong. Typically it's the intangibles that make a difference. These include:

- *Parents feeling part of a caring community*—How connected are parents to other adults and other parents in your congregation? Do parents feel they have people they can turn to in good times and bad? This keeps parents from falling into Finding #1: going it alone and Finding #4: feeling overwhelmed by challenges.
- *Parents being nurtured and supported*—How does your congregation help parents grow? How are marriages and parent partnerships strengthened? How are parents nurtured to be even more successful as parents? This focuses on Finding #2: most parents lack a strong parenting partner and Finding #3: many parents feel successful as parents most of the time.
- *Parents being the recipients of small, helpful gestures*—How do congregational leaders and members help out parents in small ways? When a young child begins to misbehave during a worship service, how do adults try to help the parent? (Or does the parent feel scolded and shamed?) How often do adults in your congregation interact with children and teenagers so that young people know other adults besides their parents? This ties into Finding #5: small things make a big difference for parents.

Effective programs can make a difference for parents, but effective programs are only one piece of the puzzle in helping parents. Parents need time to get to know other parents and other adults in your congregation. But how do you do that if a parent attends only a worship service for an hour each week and participates in nothing else that your congregation offers? How do you help parents connect with each other if your programming is only about training or educating them?

Create structures so parents have time to connect with one another. Build in time for parents to talk (such as assigning them a conversation starter) during an educational activity. Form support groups for parents. A survey of individuals in support groups found that the main reason people participated in these groups was they "made you feel like you weren't alone."[9]

105

Your Congregation's Influence

As you build on your congregation's strengths while supporting and equipping parents, you'll create a climate that's welcoming to parents and their children. In times like these, congregations cannot afford to continue losing members while having the remaining members grow so old. Asset building not only supports and equips parents, but it also reignites the spark that keeps your congregation burning bright.

Everyone succeeds when a congregation adopts the asset approach. The parents thrive. Their children and youth grow up well. Your congregation grows. Asset building is a strategy that works.

Chapter 7

Unleashing the Power of Your Congregation and Those Involved

IN HELPING PARENTS, it's important to tap into the power of individuals, groups, and your congregation as a whole. Congregational leaders and members are often uncomfortable with the concept of power, but we're not advocating a power that controls and dictates. Instead, there are positive aspects of power, such as the power that unleashes the gifts and talents of individuals, groups, and your congregation to make a positive difference in the lives of parents and their children.

The Power of Your Congregational Leadership

People in your congregation look to your leadership for guidance and direction. When your leadership is on board with helping parents and making parents a priority, your members are more likely to join in and participate.

Although your congregational leaders may not be involved in the work of planning how to help parents or implementing those plans, it's essential that they be fully aware and supportive of what you're doing. Congregational leaders are often pulled in many directions at the same time, and they are busy. Finding ways to keep them informed and involved is critical to how effective you will be in helping parents.

As you keep congregational leaders informed, make sure that you're viewing them as true partners in your work. Although you may be doing most of the legwork, their insights can be very helpful. When other congregational leaders feel heard and involved in the process (even if it seems small to you), they will be more likely to advocate for parents and to speak to other influential people about what you're doing.

In one congregation, the council president was resistant to helping parents because he was a parent and he didn't need any help. Members of the congregation continued working with him and encouraging him to provide his insight, even though his insight only seemed to question the entire notion of helping parents.

Then the council president began having difficulty with his teenage son. His son no longer

---

A CONGREGATION SUCCESS STORY

Supporting Parents

At Prince of Peace Lutheran Church in Carrollton, Texas, congregation leaders used the visual of building blocks for a sermon illustration to introduce the congregation to asset building. Pastor Kenneth Holdorf made 40 building blocks out of two-by-fours and wrote one of the developmental assets on each block along with Bible passages that correspond with each developmental asset. He made a cross as the foundation and asked kids from the congregation to come up and stand on the blocks. He then asked the congregation, "Are you committed to building up the lives of our young people?"

Because he knows that parents are key to helping young people grow up well, he is making a simple shack out of two-by-fours, which sits right outside the narthex. (He says this shack will never be finished because the work of building assets is never finished.) He is putting the building blocks inside the shack and placing free handouts for parents and other adults to take.

Principles of Asset Building

Six principles guide the work of asset building, and these six principles help you keep the larger picture of asset building in mind as you help parents.

1. **Relationships are key**—To be successful, the asset approach calls upon *all* members of a congregation to build both formal and informal, positive, caring relationships not only with children and teenagers but also with their parents. Learning people's names and getting to know them is essential in building relationships, as are mentoring programs.

2. **Everyone can build assets**—Parents can build assets in their children, but parents cannot build assets alone. Everyone can build assets: your congregational leadership, the members of your congregation, your Christian education teachers, your volunteers. Everyone has something to contribute.

3. **Delivering consistent messages is critical**—While it's important for parents to treat their children with respect, those attitudes can be undermined when others in worship, in Christian education classes, or during fellowship times don't do the same. Thus it's important that we begin rallying everyone in the congregation to recognize his or her role and responsibility.

4. **All children and teenagers need assets**—Sometimes it's easy for a congregation to focus on those who seem "at risk" or may need extra help. Although, these young people need their assets built, so do all the children and teenagers in our congregation and community. All parents need support in building assets in their children, and parents need important partners who also will build assets in their children.

5. **Asset building is an ongoing process**—Asset building isn't a one-year emphasis that stops when the year is over. Infants grow into toddlers who advance to preschoolers

who become elementary-age children who then enter the teenage years. Young people need their assets built every step of the way, and parents need our support and involvement during this important journey.

6. Duplication and repetition are necessary—Our society views the words duplication and repetition as negative, and we tend to interpret these actions as inefficient and costly. Yet young people and their parents should receive multiple exposure to the developmental assets through your congregation. You can't assume that all parents are building all the developmental assets in their children, which is why your members also need to build assets. That way, if kids are having their assets built at home, they will be getting more help. Those who aren't, are at least getting their assets built through your congregation.

wanted to go to church. Gradually the council president realized what an impact the congregation could have had on his son if he hadn't been so resistant and had encouraged other adults to get to know his son. For the first time, he began to see the importance of intergenerational relationships that a congregation can provide when congregational members are intentional about creating those relationships. From that point on, he was on board, and he became a strong advocate.

If you're using the developmental asset approach to helping parents, make the following key points about how asset building fits with the mission and emphases of your congregation.

• *Asset building is at the heart of what we do in our congregation*—Asset building is not another program or task force emphasis. It's about equipping parents and children so that they can be the best Christians they can be. It's about building a strong community within our congregation so that everyone feels that he or she belongs. It's about bringing out the best in each individual member.

RESEARCH INSIGHTS

Showing Parents Why Your Congregation Helps Kids Succeed

You can make the case to parents that your congregation is essential in raising successful kids. When Search Institute researchers compared the number of assets of religiously active young people with those who are inactive or not religious, they found that young people who spend at least an hour each week going to programs, groups, or services at a congregation were more likely to have each of the 40 developmental assets.[1]

	Percentage of Religiously Active Young People	Percentage of Inactive or Non-Religious Young People
Support		
#1: Family support	75%	62%
#2: Positive family communication	35%	23%
#3: Other adult relationships	50%	35%
#4: Caring neighborhood	46%	30%
#5: Caring school climate	34%	22%
#6: Parental involvement in schooling	38%	26%
Empowerment		
#7: Community values youth	29%	17%
#8: Youth as resources	33%	21%
#9: Service to others	60%	36%
#10: Safety	50%	53%
Boundaries and Expectations		
#11: Family boundaries	53%	39%
#12: School boundaries	56%	48%
#13: Neighborhood boundaries	53%	42%
#14: Adult role models	35%	20%

#15: Positive peer influence	71%	55%
#16: High expectations	53%	42%
Constructive Use of Time		
#17: Creative activities	24%	15%
#18: Youth programs	67%	45%
#19: Religious community*	*	*
#20: Time at home	54%	48%
Commitment to Learning		
#21: Achievement motivation	72%	59%
#22: School engagement	65%	55%
#23: Homework	56%	47%
#24: Bonding to school	59%	45%
#25: Reading for pleasure	25%	19%
Positive Values		
#26: Caring	56%	41%
#27: Equality and social justice	56%	45%
#28: Integrity	71%	63%
#29: Honesty	71%	60%
#30: Responsibility	67%	57%
#31: Restraint	55%	33%
Social Competencies		
#32: Planning and decision making	33%	25%
#33: Interpersonal competence	51%	39%
#34: Cultural competence	45%	37%
#35: Resistance skills	46%	33%
#36: Peaceful conflict resolution	50%	37%
Positive Identity		
#37: Personal power	47%	39%
#38: Self-esteem	54%	47%
#39: Sense of purpose	63%	53%
#40: Positive view of personal future	77%	68%

* This asset is the basis for distinguishing between religious and nonreligious/inactive young people.

• *Asset building fits with our congregation's mission*—Take the mission of your congregation and draw connections between it and the principles of asset building. See the box "Principles of Asset Building."

• *Many congregations are making asset building a priority*—This isn't something new for congregations. There are a number of congregations across the country that are asset-rich

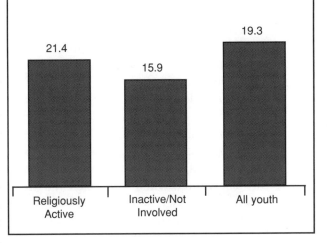

RESEARCH INSIGHTS

Levels of Developmental Assets

Young people who are active in a congregation (by attending at least once a week), have more developmental assets (on average) than young people who are not involved in a congregation.[2]

21.4   15.9   19.3

Religiously Active   Inactive/Not Involved   All youth

congregations. Many denominational conferences and annual meetings now include something about asset building. For example, the U.S. Conference of Catholic Bishops 1997 pastoral letter on youth ministry emphasizes asset-building approaches in their parishes.[3] *The Lutheran* magazine devoted an issue to asset building.[4] Leaders in the Evangelical Lutheran Church in America and the Lutheran Church–Missouri Synod use developmental assets as a lens for planning national events and initiatives. Several conferences of the United Methodist Church as well as regional groups from other denominations have offered training

113

to congregations on using developmental assets in their ministries.

• *Asset building helps us attract new members and retain those who come*—Many parents in your community are looking for congregations that have meaningful activities for their children and themselves. They want to connect with principled people and have their children get to know them. Asset building often adds new life to a congregation and gets people excited about coming.

The Power of Individuals

Researchers agree that one caring adult can make a difference in a child's life,[5] and one adult may be the critical lifeline that a parent needs at a certain time. Each person within your congregation (whether he or she is a member or a congregational leader) has the power to influence parents and their children. The influence may seem small or insignificant; but these small, daily acts make a difference.

A parent can feel less alone when someone in your congregation calls him or her by name and says hello. A parent can feel wanted when someone calls the parent on the phone to say she missed seeing this parent at worship services. A parent can feel supported when someone offers to hold the baby or play briefly with a toddler while the parent goes to the bathroom. These small gestures help parents open up and build relationships with others.

Over time as relationships develop, people in your congregation often influence parents without knowing it. A conversation about work can sometimes alter the career plans for a parent in a positive way. An older person remembering having a secretive teenager can help a parent of a teenager see that someone understands and has been there before. A member who invites a child to a community play or community sporting event can give a stressed-out parent a much-needed break.

The Power of Parents

Parents are "the most influential adults in children's lives," even when kids are at school, at a soccer practice, or any other place away from home.[6] Parents create a home environment that either brings out the best in their children or hinders their development. Parents are the ones who help their children choose which activities to participate in or not take part in any program. Parents are the ones who take their children to your congregation or let them sleep in and not attend at all.

Parents often need to be reminded of how much influence they have, particularly when their children enter the teenage years and assert their independence. They need to see that the small positive actions that they're doing actually help—even if they can't see the difference right now. This may be why so many parents said in our study that it helps to have

A CONGREGATION SUCCESS STORY

A Congregation That Shares High Expectations with Parents

Many parents expect a lot of their kids, and congregational leaders at Mount Gideon Missionary Baptist Church in St. Louis, Missouri, do too. The congregation sponsors a program to recognize outstanding young people in the community through membership in "Youth on a Mission." Young people can be in the program if they:

- Maintain a grade-point average of at least 3.25;
- Submit a letter of reference from both a teacher and the pastor of their congregation; and
- Participate in a monthly community service project.

The rigorous membership requirements are an incentive for local young people to work hard in their homes, their school, their congregation, and their community. Parents appreciate the emphasis on academic achievement and service from this congregation.

other people say something about the good things they do. Parents in the daily throes of life often don't see the results of their efforts until years later.

To support parents, show them how your congregation is an important partner for them. Search Institute studies show that young people who participate in a congregation are more likely to have more developmental assets than those who do not participate. See the research insights, "Showing Parents Why Your Congregation Helps Kids Succeed" and "Levels of Developmental Assets." Download the one-page handout to give parents this information.[7] Point out how young people in congregations are more likely to have all of the developmental assets[8] and that some there are significant differences with a number of the assets, such as asset #18: youth programs and asset #31: restraint.

"Asset-rich kids are more willing to take a path that is considered spiritual or religious," says Peter Benson, president of Search Institute who developed the developmental asset framework. "They are more able to be reflective and go deeper, be hopeful, express gratitude, celebration, thankfulness. They have a sense of purpose."[9]

Parents do have a lot of influence on their children, but reiterate how parents cannot—and should not—raise good kids alone. Your congregation is a partner, just like the individuals in your congregation are partners. Schools, coaches, neighbors, libraries, pediatricians, and communities are just a few of the countless partners that parents have.

The Power of Groups

Most likely you have a number of groups within your congregation. These may be men's groups, women's groups, and other groups. These groups may not have a lot of influence on your congregation's planning and decision-making process, but they do have a lot of influence on individuals, particularly parents.

How do these groups include parents? Sometimes these groups can become age segregated and inadvertently exclude people of certain ages. In a number of congregations, a mom's group isn't for all moms, it's only for stay-at-home moms of young children. Be mindful about these circumstances to ensure that parents have groups they can become a part of.

Sometimes it's helpful to create new groups so that parents have a place to belong. After the birth of her child with Down Syndrome, one mother felt isolated and disconnected from other parents. When she found other parents who had a child with Down Syndrome, everything changed for her. "It wasn't until I connected with a family who had a child a year and half older than my own that all the walls came down," she says. "My feelings were lightened by someone who really and truly knew what I was going through."

This is what you want your parents to find: other parents who really and truly know what they're going through. The difficulty today is that there are so many specific parenting issues, that you need to know who your parents are before you can create some of these groups. For example, congregations have created support groups around the age of kids, whether parents are stay-at-home parents or working parents, and the type of family they have (two-parent families, single-parent families, blended families, adoptive families, foster families, and so on). There are countless other issues, such as parents of preemies, vegetarian parents, parents dealing with specific medical issues for themselves and/or their children, and parents who also are caring for their elderly or sick parents. It doesn't matter what type of groups you create, what matters is that you create meaningful groups that help parents connect to other parents and want to keep coming back for more.

The Power of Informal Relationships

Many congregations are becoming more intentional about creating informal relationships. In the past, congregations didn't need to do this because people had the time to mingle and find people on their own. With our fast-paced society, this option doesn't exist, even if you do have fellowship and social gatherings.

Ten years ago, we belonged to a congregation that was open to the idea of connecting adults with kids. We developed an informal program called Faith Partners.[10] The requirements were simple: If you were interested in getting to know someone else in the congregation, you could sign up. Teenagers were asked if they wanted to be linked with an adult in the congregation, or if they wanted to connect with a younger child. The commitment was for a school year (from September to May), and all you needed to do was to meet your faith partner and get to know him or her.

A CONGREGATION SUCCESS STORY

Connecting Kids with Other Congregational Adults

In Mesa, Arizona, Grace United Methodist Church has a faith-mentoring program where young people and other adults in the congregation are paired together. They exchange photographs and pray for each other. The congregation does this for 16 weeks each spring, so that the program ends when the confirmation program ends. "When a young person gets confirmed, there is much more of a rejoicing of the whole congregation," says Carol Harris of the congregation. Because so many adults have been mentors, many know the confirmands personally. A number of the adults not only stayed with the young people during the 16 weeks but also attended their school events and graduations, cheering them on every step of the way.

We separated the adults from the kids and then started making matches. Usually we had more kids than adults, so sometimes we recruited more adults or asked some adults if they would be interested in having two faith partners. Then we mailed each person his or her new faith partner and let them find each other.

Some partners really got to know each other. They invited each other's family over for dinner or got together for some other outing. They celebrated birthdays together, and became significant supports for each other. Others matched a name with a face and started greeting each other on a regular basis. Sometimes they sat together during a worship service or talked briefly during a fellowship time.

Each September, we started from scratch. That way more adults and kids could get to know more people, and slowly a stronger sense of community was built.

A number of other congregations do this type of informal pairing in different ways. At Bethany Lutheran Church in Iowa Falls, Iowa, the congregation pairs children in the after-school program with adults in the congregation. The children call their adults "their guardian angels" and they attend a banquet together at the end of the school year. First Presbyterian Church in Knoxville, Tennessee, provides music lessons for children and teenagers who otherwise cannot afford them. Each of the 40 young people who receive music lessons also are paired with an adult artist/mentor from the congregation or community.[11] Another congregation created "faith grandpas" and "faith grandmas" for families whose extended families live far away, are deceased, or are not involved in their lives. Two congregations in Chicago started a pen pal program where one adult member from a congregation was matched with a young person in another congregation.

The Power of Programs

Our findings from the survey with 1,005 parents revealed that informal relationships and supports are often more valued by parents than formal programs. Yet, all congregations have programs, and our findings suggest ways to make your programs even more effective for helping parents.

• *Examine your existing programs*—Which of your existing programs have a high participation of parents? Which
don't have any parents involved? Why is this? Sometimes
parents don't participate because they don't know about
your programs, the programs occur at inconvenient times for
them, the programs are irrelevant for parents, or the programs require a lot of work without giving much in return.
Ask parents for honest feedback about your programs.

Some parents also find that certain congregational programs welcome them because they want parent volunteers,
such as educational programs and youth programs. Yet parents may shrink back from these opportunities because they
clearly see what's expected: for parents to give. Which programs does your congregation have that help parents connect
with other parents and allow them to contribute in meaningful ways (in ways that parents want to, not just the way your
congregation wants parents to)? How can you enhance your
current programs so that they address one if not more of the
five findings of our study?

Some parents may be interested in a number of your
congregational programs, but the way these programs are
currently designed keep parents from participating. A
congregational choir may interest parents, but some parents
may not be able to make the commitment of a weekly
rehearsal and performance due to a lack of child care. Or parents may not have that kind of time. One congregation dealt
with this difficulty by creating a family choir in addition to
the congregation's other choir. The family choir (which was
open to parents and children of all ages) rehearsed once a
month and sang for worship services twice a year.

No matter which programs your congregation offers,
encourage program leaders to make their programs more
effective by creating ways for participants to connect with
one another and build deep relationships. Maybe adding a
community-building activity or having conversation starters
would begin the process for participants to get to know one
another.

Look beyond the programs that cater directly to parents and young people. Also consider how your programs for music, service, mission, congregational care, and administration can identify concrete ways to help parents feel more part of your congregation.

• *Develop new programs*—Sometimes the findings from our study of parents or the developmental asset framework trigger new ideas for congregational leaders, and they begin to develop something they had never imagined. Bethel Lutheran Church in Northfield, Minnesota, developed an intergenerational summer Bible school. Adults learned side by side with children and teenagers. In addition to scripture studies, the program also built relationships between children, teenagers, and adults.

At Glen Mar United Methodist Church in Elliott City, Maryland, congregational leaders developed little cards that included ways people reach out to children, youth, and parents in the congregation. Each card included a simple way to reach out to other people (such as learning their names or making eye contact with them and smiling) and also included a supporting scripture verse.[12]

The Wings Ministry in Albuquerque, New Mexico, created an even more intensive program where the congregation hosts three parties each year for families of inmates. A different local congregation hosts each event, and congregational members come together to support the families at parties. "With Wings, you can't tell who is a member of the church and who has a family member in prison," says Ann Edenfield, who created this ministry. The family members who come often comment about how surprised they are that congregational people can be so much fun.

The Power of Your Congregation

As a congregation, you have been called to be God's hands and feet in our world. How will you do that for parents and their children? The Lutheran Church of the Reformation in St. Louis Park, Minnesota, focused on one developmental asset per week, tying the asset into the lectionary lesson. Sometimes the sermon was based on the asset and sometimes a parent, a family, or a lay leader gave a short presentation on the asset during the worship service. The congregation then started a low-cost babysitting service for parents and also offered space for home-schooling parents and their children.[13]

Heritage Presbyterian Church in Glendale, Arizona, decorated their sanctuary with silhouettes of children and teenagers from the congregation. Each silhouette had a heart and a sentence that the young person wrote to describe himself or herself. Another congregation had each adult, parent, and young person trace their hands, cut them out, place their hands, cut them out, place their name on the hand, and hang their hands in the sanctuary to illustrate the importance of each person and the hands we have to hold each other and to help each other.

Not only do the five findings of our study on 1,005 parents show the importance of congregations, but so do other studies as well. Researchers investigating the strengths, stresses, and faith practices of congregational families also concluded, "how important it is for the church community to come alongside parents and take seriously that children are the responsibility of the community, and that all adults in the community of faith have a role to play."[14]

Congregations will be most effective in helping parents when they see themselves as true partners. A congregation will have an even greater impact when individuals do their part in creating a caring community that truly supports parents. How will your congregation help parents? How will the individuals in your congregations discover the unique ways they can connect to parents and help them? These are the questions worth pondering. These are the questions that when answered well can transform your congregation into a welcoming, nurturing haven for parents and their children.

Resources

ANY RESOURCES give an overview of family ministry, but many family ministry resources overlook parents. We have highlighted a few key resources that either help you nurture parents or give you practical advice on how to build developmental assets in your congregation. These include:

A Scientific, Low-Cost Survey of Your Congregation

• **Building Assets, Strengthening Faith: An Intergenerational Survey for Congregations,** by Search Institute, is a comprehensive survey for youth (grades six and older) and adults who are part of your congregation. This easy-to-use survey (which is also available in large print), provides in-depth information that helps your leaders plan for your congregation's future. Available through Search Institute, Minneapolis, www.search-institute.org/congregations.

Asset-Building Resources for Congregations

• **Building Assets in Congregations,** by Eugene Roehlkepartain, presents an overview of how to transform your entire congregation into an asset-building congregation. This practical book includes worksheets for assessing and planning your current priorities and programs, tips for creating intergenerational programs and parent workshops, and ten reproducible bulletin inserts. Available through Search Institute, Minneapolis.
• **Ideas for Parents,** by Jolene Roehlkepartain, is a 52-newsletter master set that you can photocopy and distribute to parents. Each two-page newsletter introduces one of the developmental assets (or one of the asset categories) and gives parents ideas for how to talk with their kids, how

to build assets in their children, and where to get more in-depth information about asset building. Available through Search Institute, Minneapolis.

Resources for Developing a Cutting-Edge Family Ministry

• **Family Ministry: A Comprehensive Guide,** by Diana R. Garland, makes the case that congregations can do even more to strengthen family relationships. This 629-page book is truly comprehensive, covering all aspects of congregational life. Available through InterVarsity Press, Downers Grove, Illinois.

• **A New Day for Family Ministry,** by Richard P. Olson and Joe H. Leonard, Jr., presents the strong argument that family ministries need to adapt to the cultural shifts that have changed many aspects of family life. It also suggests ways for congregations to make themselves more family friendly. Available through the Alban Institute, Bethesda, Maryland.

• **Nurturing Faith in Families,** by Jolene Roehlkepartain, gives 425 creative ideas for family ministry. What's unique about this book, however, is that is shows how to integrate families into all aspects of congregational life from music to worship and from education to service. Available through Abingdon Press, Nashville.

A Journal to Keep Up with the Cutting Edge of Family Ministry

Family Ministry, a quarterly journal published by Louisville Presbyterian Theological Seminary, provides provocative articles about family ministry, snapshots of successful congregations doing family ministry, and cutting-edge information about family ministry. Contact *Family Ministry* at 1044 Alta Vista Road, Louisville, KY 40205-1798, email: family@fmef.org or visit the Web site at www.fmef.org.

Appendix

40 Assets Infants Need to Succeed

[Birth to 12 Months]

Search Institute has identified a framework of 40 developmental assets for infants from birth to 12 months that blends Search Institute's research on developmental assets for 12- to 18-year-olds with the extensive literature in child development. For the definitions to each of these 40 developmental assets for infants, go to www.search-institute.org/assets/40Assets-Infants.pdf. To build assets in infants, see *What Young Children Need to Succeed* (published by Free Spirit in 2000).

External Assets

Support
1. Family support
2. Positive family communication
3. Other adult relationships
4. Caring neighborhood
5. Caring out-of-home climate
6. Parent involvement in out-of-home situations

Empowerment
7. Community values children
8. Children are given useful roles
9. Service to others
10. Safety

Boundaries and Expectations
11. Family boundaries
12. Out-of-home boundaries
13. Neighborhood boundaries
14. Adult role models
15. Positive peer observation
16. Appropriate expectations for growth

Constructive Use of Time
17. Creative activities
18. Out-of-home activities
19. Religious community
20. Positive, supervised time at home

Internal Assets

Commitment to Learning
21. Achievement expectation and motivation
22. Children are engaged in learning
23. Stimulating activity
24. Enjoyment of learning
25. Reading for pleasure

Positive Values
26. Family values caring
27. Family values equality and social justice
28. Family values integrity
29. Family values honesty
30. Family values responsibility
31. Family values healthy lifestyle

Social Competencies
32. Planning and decision making observation
33. Interpersonal skills observation
34. Cultural observation
35. Resistance observation
36. Peaceful conflict resolution observation

Positive Identity
37. Family has personal power
38. Family models high self-esteem
39. Family has a sense of purpose
40. Family has a positive view of the future

40 Assets Toddlers Need to Succeed

[Ages 13 to 35 Months]

Search Institute has identified a framework of 40 developmental assets for toddlers from 13 to 35 months that blends Search Institute's research on developmental assets for 12- to 18-year-olds with the extensive literature in child development. For the definitions to each of these 40 developmental assets for toddlers, go to www.search-institute.org/assets/40Assets-Toddlers.pdf. To build assets in toddlers, see *What Young Children Need to Succeed* (published by Free Spirit in 2000).

External Assets

Support
1. Family support
2. Positive family communication
3. Other adult relationships
4. Caring neighborhood
5. Caring out-of-home climate
6. Parent involvement in out-of-home situations

Empowerment
7. Community values children
8. Children are given useful roles
9. Service to others
10. Safety

Boundaries and Expectations
11. Family boundaries
12. Out-of-home boundaries
13. Neighborhood boundaries
14. Adult role models
15. Positive peer observation
16. Appropriate expectations for growth

Constructive Use of Time
17. Creative activities
18. Out-of-home activities
19. Religious community
20. Positive, supervised time at home

Internal Assets

Commitment to Learning
21. Achievement expectation and motivation
22. Children are engaged in learning
23. Stimulating activity
24. Enjoyment of learning
25. Reading for pleasure

Positive Values
26. Family values caring
27. Family values equality and social justice
28. Family values integrity
29. Family values honesty
30. Family values responsibility
31. Family values healthy lifestyle

Social Competencies
32. Planning and decision making observation
33. Interpersonal observation
34. Cultural observation
35. Resistance observation
36. Peaceful conflict resolution observation

Positive Identity
37. Family has personal power
38. Family models high self-esteem
39. Family has a sense of purpose
40. Family has a positive view of the future

40 Assets Preschoolers Need to Succeed

[Ages 3 to 5 Years]

Search Institute has identified a framework of 40 developmental assets for preschoolers from 3 to 5 years that blends Search Institute's research on developmental assets for 12- to 18-year-olds with the extensive literature in child development. For the definitions to each of these 40 developmental assets for preschoolers, go to www.search-institute.org/assets/40Assets-Preschoolers.pdf. To build assets in preschoolers, see *What Young Children Need to Succeed* (published by Free Spirit in 2000).

External Assets

Support
1. Family support
2. Positive family communication
3. Other adult relationships
4. Caring neighborhood
5. Caring out-of-home climate
6. Parent involvement in out-of-home situations

Empowerment
7. Community values children
8. Children are given useful roles
9. Service to others
10. Safety

Boundaries and Expectations
11. Family boundaries
12. Out-of-home boundaries
13. Neighborhood boundaries
14. Adult role models
15. Positive peer interactions
16. Appropriate expectations for growth

Constructive Use of Time
17. Creative activities
18. Out-of-home activities
19. Religious community
20. Positive, supervised time at home

Internal Assets

Commitment to Learning
21. Achievement expectation and motivation
22. Children are engaged in learning
23. Stimulating activity
24. Enjoyment of learning
25. Reading for pleasure

Positive Values
26. Family values caring
27. Family values equality and social justice
28. Family values integrity
29. Family values honesty
30. Family values responsibility
31. Family values healthy lifestyle

Social Competencies
32. Planning and decision making practice
33. Interpersonal interactions
34. Cultural interactions
35. Resistance practice
36. Peaceful conflict resolution practice

Positive Identity
37. Family has personal power
38. Family models high self-esteem
39. Family has a sense of purpose
40. Family has a positive view of the future

40 Assets Elementary-Age Children Need to Succeed

[Ages 6 to 11 Years]

Search Institute has identified a framework of 40 developmental assets for elementary-age children from 6 to 11 years that blends Search Institute's research on developmental assets for 12- to 18-year-olds with the extensive literature in child development. For the definitions to each of these 40 developmental assets for elementary-age children, go to www.search-institute.org/assets/40Assets-Elementary.pdf. To build assets in 6- to 11-year-olds, see *What Young Children Need to Succeed* (published by Free Spirit in 2000).

External Assets

Support
1. Family support
2. Positive family communication
3. Other adult relationships
4. Caring neighborhood
5. Caring out-of-home climate
6. Parent involvement in out-of-home situations

Empowerment
7. Community values children
8. Children are given useful roles
9. Service to others
10. Safety

Boundaries and Expectations
11. Family boundaries
12. Out-of-home boundaries
13. Neighborhood boundaries
14. Adult role models
15. Positive peer interaction and influence
16. Appropriate expectations for growth

Constructive Use of Time
17. Creative activities
18. Out-of-home activities
19. Religious community
20. Positive, supervised time at home

Internal Assets

Commitment to Learning
21. Achievement expectation and motivation
22. Children are engaged in learning
23. Stimulating activity and homework
24. Enjoyment of learning and bonding to school
25. Reading for pleasure

Positive Values
26. Caring
27. Equality and social justice
28. Integrity
29. Honesty
30. Responsibility
31. Healthy lifestyle and sexual attitudes

Social Competencies
32. Planning and decision making
33. Interpersonal skills
34. Cultural competence
35. Resistance skills
36. Peaceful conflict resolution

Positive Identity
37. Personal power
38. Self-esteem
39. Sense of purpose
40. Positive view of personal future

40 Assets Middle and High School Young People Need to Succeed

[Ages 12 to 18 Years]

Search Institute has identified the following building blocks that help young people grow up healthy, caring, and responsible. For the definitions to each of these 40 developmental assets for young people, go to our Web site www.search-institute.org/assets/40Assets.pdf. To build assets in 12- to 18-year-olds, see *What Kids Need to Succeed* (published by Free Spirit in 1998).

External Assets

Support
1. Family support
2. Positive family communication
3. Other adult relationships
4. Caring neighborhood
5. Caring school climate
6. Parent involvement in schooling

Empowerment
7. Community values youth
8. Youth as resources
9. Service to others
10. Safety

Boundaries and Expectations
11. Family boundaries
12. School boundaries
13. Neighborhood boundaries
14. Adult role models
15. Positive peer influence
16. High expectations

Constructive Use of Time
17. Creative activities
18. Youth programs
19. Religious community
20. Time at home

Internal Assets

Commitment to Learning
21. Achievement motivation
22. School engagement
23. Homework
24. Bonding to school
25. Reading for pleasure

Positive Values
26. Caring
27. Equality and social justice
28. Integrity
29. Honesty
30. Responsibility
31. Restraint

Social Competencies
32. Planning and decision-making
33. Interpersonal competence
34. Cultural competence
35. Resistance skills
36. Peaceful conflict resolution

Positive Identity
37. Personal power
38. Self-esteem
39. Sense of purpose
40. Positive view of personal future

Connecting Assets to Scripture

The scripture passages listed below can serve as spring-boards for reflecting on the potential connections between biblical texts and each of the 40 developmental assets identified by Search Institute.

Asset	Old Testament	New Testament
1. Family Support	Psalm 103:13-14	Ephesians 5:1-2
2. Positive Family Communication	Deuteronomy 6:4-9; Proverbs 15:1-4	Ephesians 4:15-16; Ephesians 6:4
3. Other Adult Relationships	2 Samuel 9:1-13; 2 Kings 2	2 Timothy 1:1-14
4. Caring Neighborhood	Leviticus 19:18, 33-34	Mark 12:31-33
5. Caring School Climate	Ezekiel 34:11-15	Mark 9:37
6. Parent Involvement in Schooling	Proverbs 22:6	Luke 2:41-52
7. Community Values Youth	Jeremiah 1:5-8	Luke 15:1-10; Matthew 19:13-15
8. Youth as Resources	1 Samuel 16:1	Timothy 4:12; Romans 12:4-8
9. Service to Others	Isaiah 6	Romans 12:9-13
10. Safety	Psalm 12:6-8	Luke 15:1-7
11. Family Boundaries	Exodus 20:12; Proverbs 29:17	Hebrews 12:5-13; Ephesians 6:1-4
12. School Boundaries	Proverbs 13:13	Titus 3:1-2
13. Neighborhood Boundaries	Leviticus 19:15-18	Ephesians 4:25-28
14. Adult Role Models	1 Samuel 3	Matthew 1:18-25; Hebrews 11, 13:7
15. Positive Peer Influence	1 Samuel 20	Philippians 2:1-5
16. High Expectations	Exodus 3-4	2 Thessalonians 3:6-13
17. Creative Activities	Psalms 148-150	Ephesians 5:19-20
18. Youth Programs	Ecclesiastes 3:1, 17	2 Corinthians 10:15-18
19. Religious Community	Isaiah 35:1-10	Acts 2:46-47

20. Time at Home	Ruth 1:16-18	Luke 15:11-32
21. Achievement Motivation	Nehemiah 2:11-18	Hebrews 12:1-2
22. School Engagement	Exodus 31:1-5; Psalm 119:33-40	Colossians 3:23-24
23. Homework	Ezra 7:8-10	Luke 19:11-27
24. Bonding to School	Psalm 27:11	Romans 13:1-3
25. Reading for Pleasure	Jeremiah 36:1-10	Acts 15:22-35
26. Caring	2 Kings 5:1-3, 7-15	Luke 10:25-37
27. Equality and Social Justice	Isaiah 42:6-7; Amos 5:24	Matthew 25:34-36; Luke 16:19-31
28. Integrity	Micah 6:8	2 Thessalonians 2:1-5, 13-17
29. Honesty	Proverbs 16:13; 24:26	Luke 23:33-43
30. Responsibility	Ezekiel 18:1-9	Luke 16:1-13; Ephesians 4:1-6
31. Restraint	Numbers 25:1-5	1 Thessalonians 4:3
32. Planning and Decision Making	Isaiah 1:1-5	Luke 14:28-33
33. Interpersonal Skills	1 Samuel 20:1-17	Galatians 5:13; 1 Timothy 6:18
34. Cultural Competence	Isaiah 11:1-10	Romans 15:4-13
35. Resistance Skills	Proverbs 28:4-5	1 Corinthians 10:13
36. Peaceful Conflict Resolution	Isaiah 2:1-5	Matthew 5:9
37. Personal Power	1 Kings 17:7-16	Romans 12:1-8
38. Self-esteem	Psalm 139:13	John 8:31-36
39. Sense of Purpose	Isaiah 43:1-7	2 Timothy 4:5-11
40. Positive View of Personal Future	Jeremiah 29:11-12	Luke 6:20-31

Notes

Introduction: Making Families a Priority

1. Connect for Kids, "#72: Support Children and Families," downloaded from www.connectforkids.org/info-url1564/info-url_show.htm?doc_id=8726, on February 21, 2003.

2. The research project team consisted of 15 members from Search Institute and YMCA of the USA. In addition, we also tapped the helpful assistance of 21 project advisors who were individuals from national parenting organizations and major universities. For more information about these 36 individuals, see page 4 of *Building Strong Families: An In-Depth Report on a Preliminary Survey on What Parents Need to Succeed,* which you can download from the Web site www.search-institute.org/families.

3. This study, called *Building Strong Families,* was a 15-minute telephone poll conducted in May 2002 of 1,005 parents with children under age 18 from across the United States. The poll was conducted by Global Strategy Group on behalf of YMCA of the USA and Search Institute.

4. Diana R. Garland, "From the Editor," *Family Ministry* 16, no. 4 (Winter 2002): 7.

5. Penny Edgell Becker, "It's Not Just a Matter of Time: How the Time Squeeze Affects Congregational Participation," *Family Ministry* 15, no. 2 (Summer 2001): 23, 25.

1. Most Parents Are Going It Alone

1. U.S. Census Bureau, "No. 57. Family Groups with Children under 18 Years Old by Race and Hispanic Origin: 1980 to 2000," in *Statistical Abstract of the United States 2001* (Washington, D.C.: U.S. Census Bureau, 2001), 51. Data is taken from the 2000 Census.

2. Eugene C. Roehlkepartain, Peter C. Scales, Jolene L. Roehlkepartain, and Stacey P. Rude, *Building Strong Families: An In-Depth Report on a Preliminary Survey on What Parents Need to Succeed* (Minneapolis: Search Institute and Chicago: YMCA of the USA, 2001), 9. All other statistics that appear in this book from this study can be found in this

publication. You can download this study free of charge from the Web site www.search-institute.org/families.

3. Steve Farkas and Jean Johnson with Ann Duffett and Ali Bers, *Kids These Days: What Americans Really Think About the Next Generation* (New York: Public Agenda, 1997), 13.

4. Roehlkepartain et al., *Building Strong Families*, 9.

5. Ann Betz and Jolene L. Roehlkepartain, *Networking Congregations for Asset Building: A Tool Kit* (Minneapolis: Search Institute, 2000), 3-4.

2. Many Parents Lack a Strong Relationship with a Spouse or Partner

1. We have used the term *race* in this book to refer to the racial, ethnic, and cultural factors that could be influential on parents and their children.

2. Beverly J. Wilson and John M. Gottman, "Marital Interaction and Parenting" in Marc H. Bornstein, ed., *Handbook of Parenting, Volume 4: Applied and Practical Parenting* (Mahwah, N.J.: Erlbaum, 1995), 33-55.

3. William J. Doherty, Edward E. Kouneski, and Martha Farrell Erickson, "Responsible Fathering: An Overview and Conceptual Framework," *Journal of Marriage and the Family* 60 (1998): 277-92.

4. John Gottman and Nan Silver, *The Seven Principles for Making Marriage Work* (New York: Crown Publishers, 1999). John Gottman with Joan DeClaire, *The Heart of Parenting: How to Raise an Emotionally Intelligent Child* (New York: Simon & Schuster, 1997).

5. Linda J. Waite and Maggie Gallagher, *The Case for Marriage: Why Married People Are Happier, Healthier, and Better Off Financially* (New York: Doubleday, 2000).

6. Kristin Anderson Moore, Susan M. Jekielek, and Carol Emig, *Marriage from a Child's Perspective: How Does Family Structure Affect Children, and What Can We Do About It?* (Washington, D.C.: Child Trends, June 2002), 5-6.

7. Christian Smith and Phillip Kim, *Preliminary Findings 21: Parents in Religious Families with Teens More Likely to Express Affection or Love to Each Other*, National Study of Youth and Religion at the University of North Carolina at Chapel Hill, January 21, 2003, www.youthandreligion.org/news/2003-0121.html, downloaded February 24, 2003.

8. Smith and Kim, *Preliminary Findings 21*.

9. Ibid.

10. U.S. Census Bureau, "No. 57. Family Groups with Children under 18 Years Old by Race and Hispanic Origin: 1980 to 2000," in *Statistical Abstract of the United States 2001* (Washington, D.C.: U.S. Census Bureau, 2001), 51. Data is taken from the 2000 Census.

11. Diana Garland, "Family Ministry: Defining Perspectives," *Family Ministry* 16, no. 2 (Summer 2002): 26.

12. Gail S. Rich and Michael G. Lawler, "The First Five Years of Marriage: Resources and Programs for Ministry," *Family Ministry* 15, no. 4 (Winter 2001): 23.

13. Eugene C. Roehlkepartain, ed., *The Youth Ministry Resource Book* (Loveland, Colo.: Group Publishing, 1988), 32.

14. Jason S. Carroll and William J. Doherty, "Evaluating the Effectiveness of Premarital Prevention Programs: A Meta-Analytic Review of Outcome Research," *Family Relations* 52, no. 2 (April 2003): 105-18.

15. U.S. Bureau of Justice Statistics, *Intimate Partners Committed 20 Percent of Non-Fatal Violence Against Women in 2001,* February 23, 2003, press release (Washington, D.C.: U.S. Department of Justice, 2003). www.ojp.usdoj.gov/bjs/pub/press/ipv01pr.htm, downloaded February 24, 2003.

16. U.S. Bureau of Justice Statistics, *Crime Data Brief: Intimate Partner Violence, 1993–2001, NCJ 197838,* February 2003, highlights (Washington, D.C.: U.S. Department of Justice, 2003). www.ojp.usdoj.gov/bjs/pub/ascii/pv01pr.txt, downloaded February 24, 2003.

17. Rich and Lawler, "The First Five Years of Marriage": 23.

18. Preston Dyer and Genie Dyer, "Planning and Promoting Marriage Enrichment in the Church," *Family Ministry* 16, no. 3 (Fall 2002): 41-45.

19. U.S. Census Bureau, Current Population Survey, *Table 3: Reasons Custodial Parent Had No Legal Award, by Sex,* April 2000, www.census.gov/hhes/www/childsupport/chldsu99.pdf, downloaded February 24, 2003.

20. Peter L. Benson and Eugene C. Roehlkepartain, *Youth in Single-Parent Families: Risk and Resiliency* (Minneapolis: Search Institute, 1993), 7.

21. Ibid., 8-9.

22. See chapter 6 of this book for in-depth information on developmental assets.

23. Benson and Roehlkepartain, *Youth in Single-Parent Families,* 9.

24. Ibid.

25. Judith S. Wallerstein and Sandra Blakeslee, *Second Chances: Men, Women and Children a Decade After Divorce* (New York: Ticknor & Fields, 1989), 187.

26. Roehlkepartain et al., *Building Strong Families,* 20.

27. Ibid., 63.

28. U.S. Census Bureau, Current Population Survey, *Table 1: Child Support Payments Due and Actually Received, by Sex,* April 2000, www.census.gov/hhes/www/childsupport/chldsu99.pdf, downloaded February 24, 2003.

29. John Gottman and Nan Silver, *The Seven Principles for Making Marriage Work* (New York: Crown Publishers, 1999), 23.

3. Many Parents Feel Successful as Parents Most of the Time

1. Roehlkepartain et al., *Building Strong Families*, 29.
2. Michael J. Donahue and Peter L. Benson, "Religion and the Well-Being of Adolescent," *Journal of Social Issues* 51 (1995): 145-60.

4. Most Parents Face Ongoing Challenges

1. Lief Kehrwald, "Families and Christian Practice," *Family Ministry* 13, no. 4 (Winter 1999): 56.

5. Many Things That Would Help Parents Are Easy Things Others Can Do

1. Peter C. Scales and Nancy Leffert, *Developmental Assets* (Minneapolis: Search Institute, 1999), 21-48.
2. Peter C. Scales, Peter L. Benson, and Marc Mannes with Nancy Tellett-Royce and Jennifer Griffin-Wiesner, *Grading Grown-Ups 2002: How Do American Kids and Adults Relate? Key Findings from a National Study* (Minneapolis: Search Institute, 2002).
3. Ibid., 5.
4. Rebecca N. Saito, Theresa K. Sullivan, and Nicole R. Hintz, *The Possible Dream: What Families in Distressed Communities Need to Help Youth Thrive* (Minneapolis: Search Institute, 2000), 5.
5. Roehlkepartain et al., *Building Strong Families*. Use the study findings as a springboard for conversation, not as the final word in what you need to do in your own congregation and community, but as a conversation starter. You can download this study free of charge from the Web site www.search-institute.org/families.
6. Eugene C. Roehlkepartain, *Building Assets in Congregations: A Practical Guide for Helping Youth Grow Up Healthy* (Minneapolis: Search Institute, 1998), 171-91.

6. Equipping and Supporting Parents

1. Ann Betz and Jolene L. Roehlkepartain, *Networking Congregations for Asset Building: A Tool Kit* (Minneapolis: Search Institute, 2000), 3.
2. Arturo Sesma, Jr., and Eugene C. Roehlkepartain, "Unique Strengths, Shared Strengths: Developmental Assets Among Youth of Color," *Search Institute Insights & Evidence* 1, no. 3 (November 2003): 1-13.

3. Ibid.

4. Eugene C. Roehlkepartain, *Building Assets, Strengthening Faith: Results from a Field Test Survey of Youth and Adults in 15 U.S. Congregations* (Minneapolis: Search Institute, 2003).

5. Ibid.

6. Eugene C. Roehlkepartain, *Building Assets, Strengthening Faith: Results from a Field Test Survey of Youth and Adults in 15 U. S. Congregations* (Minneapolis: Search Institute, 2003).

7. Peter C. Scales et al., *The Attitudes and Needs of Religious Youth Workers: Perspectives from the Field* (Minneapolis: Search Institute, 1995), 15, 17, 19.

8. Eugene C. Roehlkepartain, *The Teaching Church: Moving Christian Education to Center Stage* (Nashville: Abingdon Press, 1993), 177.

9. Robert Wuthnow, *Sharing the Journey: Support Groups and America's New Quest for Community* (New York: Free Press, 1994), 170.

7. Unleashing the Power of Your Congregation and Those Involved

1. This is based on Search Institute survey data from 217,277 sixth- to twelfth-grade public school students during the 1999 to 2000 school year in public schools, the most current aggregate data set available.

2. Ibid.

3. Visit www.usccb.org/laity/youth/renewingnotes.htm for more information.

4. Visit www.thelutheran.org/9802/page8.html for more information.

5. Nancy Leffert, Peter L. Benson, and Jolene L. Roehlkepartain, *Starting Out Right: Developmental Assets for Children* (Minneapolis: Search Institute, 1997), 30.

6. National Research Council and Institute of Medicine, *From Neurons to Neighborhoods: The Science of Early Development* in Jack P. Shonkoff and Deborah Phillips, editors, Board on Children, Youth and Families, Commission on Behavior and Social Sciences and Education (Washington, D.C.: National Academy Press, 2000), 226.

7. Go to www.search-institute.org/congregations/faithandassetsresearch.html and click on the one-page reproducible chart file.

8. This is true with the exception of asset #10: safety. Although 53 percent of inactive young people have this asset and 50 percent of active young people have this asset, the 3 percent difference is not statistically significant.

9. David L. Miller, "What Do Kids Need?" *The Lutheran*, February 1998, available on the Web at www.thelutheran.org/9802/page8.html.

10. Jolene and another member of this congregation, Kris Jacobson, were instrumental in starting and running this program.

11. Jolene L. and Eugene C. Roehlkepartain, *Prescription for a Healthy Church: Ministry Ideas to Nurture Whole People* (Loveland, Colo.: Group, 2000), 63.

12. This congregation used the brochure "150 Ways to Show Kids You Care," which gives 150 easy ways to connect with kids. This brochure is available from Search Institute.

13. Ann Betz and Jolene L. Roehlkepartain, *Networking Congregations for Asset Building: A Tool Kit* (Minneapolis: Search Institute, 2000), 89-90, 115.

14. Diana R. Garland and Pamela A. Yankeelov, "The Strengths, Stresses, and Faith Practices of Congregational Families: A Research Report," *Family Ministry* 15, no. 3 (Fall 2001): 40.